Gallimaufry

Fiction, Poetry, and Reality

by Myrtle M. Burton

DORRANCE
PUBLISHING CO
EST. 1920
PITTSBURGH, PENNSYLVANIA 15238

RoseDog Books
585 Alpha Drive
Suite 103
Pittsburgh, PA 15238
Visit our website at *www.rosedogbookstore.com*

ISBN: 978-1-4809-8138-6
eISBN: 978-1-4809-8115-7

To my granddaughter,
Katrina Laura Seiser,
a special person.

Cover

The silver birch in Celtic Mythology symbolizes new beginnings and protection.

Contents

Preface

I used to frequent a lovely gift shop called "Gallimaufry." The word fascinated me, probably because it was seldom used. Even dictionary descriptions and origins give explanations that are a little fuzzy. The Oxford Dictionary describes it as *"a confused jumble or medley of things."* That description gives a delightful example: *A glorious gallimaufry of childhood perceptions.* Merriam-Webster says simply *"hodgepodge."*

My stories within are all of those things, but have been given deep thought. I am an older woman, and my hope is to reach one person or many from my experiences in a complicated world while I am able. The fiction becomes mysteries. The poetry allows me to indulge myself in proclaiming inner feelings.

The other offerings are nonfictional. All is not well with our world, and I feel a near obsession to get my thoughts out of my head and into print. A section entitled "Experiences/Opinions/Defiance" covers the realism I have known to this point in my life, even to a bitter personal experience showing how deep and lasting an experience can be.

A motif is strongly embedded in my inner psyche and appears in my writing whether or not I search for it. I deplore the destruction of our planet, atrocities of which we envision daily. Also, a new feeling of dread touches all of us. Dishonesty is now common, and for many it is accepted as normal. Injustice is thriving. Fear and greed have grown. I feel that all thinking people should talk, write, and display these travesties at every opportunity.

To begin my stories, and to heighten their merit, I offer a tribute....

I was a member of a large family growing up with a strong reverence for the natural world. My brother, Carl Burton, was a contributing influence on all of us in that respect. Father of four sons, he was a strong, muscular man with a winning personality. He also had a gentle demeanor which enhanced his persona. He had pursued forestry and parks planning in his career. The boreal forest of Canada was his panacea. However, in his professional learning and teaching he never lost sight of his talent for writing in a poetic and deeply felt realism. My literary offerings herein are presented with an introduction which follows in the form of an elegant posthumous rendering, not by me, but by him. It is entitled "The Sentinel" from my brother's heart.

The Sentinel

Carl Burton

1980

Just above our property near the mouth of Ladysmith Harbour, on Vancouver Island, there is a heavily-wooded area of second-growth cedar, and fir and hemlock. Some of the trees are festooned with dark green ivy, and emerald-coloured moss blankets the big-leaf maples. The understory of sword fern, salal and Oregon grape is punctuated in the spring with carpets of trilliums and lilies.

Scattered here and there throughout are the mouldering stumps of once-giant cedars, some still bearing the distinctive notches cut from the fallers' springboards – silent testimony to the logging carried out here a century ago.

I walk often into the sun-dappled silence of this forest, cool even on a warm July day when only the hammering of a pileated woodpecker or the plaintive peep-peep-peep of a nuthatch breaks the silence.

But the feature which most stirs me in this leafy green cathedral is a giant old-growth Douglas fir that towers far above all the other trees, a lone remnant of the original stands that clothed these hillsides that overlook the sea. Why was it alone spared? Why did it not feel the bite of the axe and the cross-cut saw and fall to the ground in a final cry of thunder?

Perhaps then, as today, it carried in its uppermost limbs a great eagle's nest of twigs and moss and branches that the fallers were loath to destroy.

I walk to this lonely giant along a narrow, shaded path. I gaze upwards in awe at the massive trunk that shoulders it way out of sight through the green canopy a hundred feet above. I place my hands on its rough and weathered bark and feel the strength of five centuries anchored in the rocky soil. I see the blackened scars from fires long past that have swept by its base, pock-marked by the drill holes of the white-shafted flickers that send small rivulets of sawdust like dry tears down its lichen-covered bark.

I talk to this silent, brooding sentinel and lean against its clean, honest coat, and it fills me with a sense of peace.

"For five hundred years you have stood vigil here. You have weathered the gales that blow in across the Strait, endured the angry hiss of lightning and the rumbling thunder, and felt the salt spray in your hair. You have stood quietly in the mist and rain and sheltered the black-tailed deer at your feet.

You have seen the dusky Salish paddlers slip out of Oyster Bay in their upswept cedar-carved canoes and heard their eerie cries echo across the water.

You have watched a hundred thousand sunsets and seen a hundred thousand dawns.

Perhaps in the distance you saw the stately Spanish ships sail quietly along the shore past Galliano and Valdes and Gabriola Islands.

You have watched as tall-masted schooners headed for home around the globe with their logs and lumber and soft coal from the Island collieries. You may have seen the ghostly grey menace of warships riding at anchor in the bay.

Now you watch the sturdy little tugboats churning up the channel with their log booms and chip barges and the Sunday sailors with their Fiberglas sailboats dancing like flocks of butterflies across the blue waters.

How many eagles have you nurtured in that eyrie? How many fledglings have tested their immature wings against the invisible currents of air and launched themselves with fierce apprehension from your lofty heights, or made awkward landings in your outstretched arms?

And now you wait in silence as ribbons of asphalt and concrete encircle you like tentacles, and sterile subdivisions and strip malls coalesce around you.

'If a tree falls in the forest,' they say, 'and no one is there to hear it, there is no sound.' When you fall, as you surely will, there will indeed be sound; it will be the sound of centuries of growing – of drawing energy from the life-giving sun, and nurture from the rain and the soil that supports you, and strength from the winds that buffet your gnarled branches. You will fall. And the eagle will hear you. And the eagle will cry."

Part I
Fiction

The Idealist

There was someone directly below when Leigh stepped silently onto the upper balcony. His business suit was not warm enough; the cold was piercing. The drapery was billowing out, unnerving. The scraping sound was muted by the howling wind.

He had fallen asleep on the sofa in waning light, drained from a long, rough flight home, when the noise awakened him. He had run up the stairs, confident that he had not been seen, and was now standing nine feet above the door from where the sound began. After a quick glance downward, he moved back inside as quietly as he could, flinching at the click of the lock. The wind would hide it.

Leigh, self-assured and charming, had made light of his friends' concern when they questioned his desire to spend dark nights alone by the lake, seven miles from the nearest commercial corner. They avoided mentioning the crime that had taken place only a dozen miles or so from his place. Always jovial, Leigh pretended shock.

"What's the big deal?" he said. "We walk through the woods and trails by day without a care. At home we leave doors unlocked in daylight, but night makes us edgy and uptight in the same places. What's to fear? I will welcome the sounds of nature and the noisy surf when it moves in by day...or by night. Besides, the crime that's on your mind was not on my beach and it's now history." With a cheeky grin he added, "I will promise to lock up good and tight every night just so you guys don't worry about me."

The earlier crime was well known; everybody was aware and troubled by it, even after almost a year, although it had been decided that the perpetrator had moved on. The figure had been preying on people living in the affluent beachfront homes, watching the movements of the residents until they let down their guard. The intruder had been a heavyset man and a real pro. He had known how to disable alarms and motion detectors. It was one crime only that resulted in death of the victim. He left no trace after finding a woman alone on her back patio. She was taken by surprise and tried to fight him off, but was pushed down a concrete stairway and left unconscious. A neighbor had found her too late. He had heard the screech of a car leaving at high speed and became suspicious. The woman, suffering from a fractured skull, was failing before the ambulance arrived. While she lay unconscious, the intruder had ransacked her home and fled. The woman passed away without gaining consciousness. Had she been tended to immediately she probably could have pulled through.

The dark interior of Leigh's beach house obviously had given the intruder the impression that nobody was at home. He had left his car in the shop before he flew to Houston, and he had not rented a car, utilizing taxis all the way.

Leigh waited. The scraping sound had stopped. On the split-level stairway he held a rifle. A weak night light offered some help. The patio door was now being opened, the deadbolt lock obviously severed. In an alcove that gave a full view of the party room, Leigh was able to see the intruder's form—a man with a hood and a handgun entering slowly, moving closer before looking upward. In the dim light their eyes met. The handgun was quickly raised. A shot went wild because the rifle had been at the ready and had been aimed toward the intruder's chest.

Leigh's trauma would always be a part of him, and he was saddened to know that the admiration he had for the exquisite gifts of wilderness would always be questioned. He learned that independence is difficult in our day. Unfettered complacency had become a luxury.

Please Come

"Please stay."

"I have to…."

"Please stay. Just for tonight."

"Lila is coming home, uh, tomorrow."

"Morning is okay. The sky gets light. Please stay. For Bianca."

Catherine saw torment in Mary's eyes. No, it was fear. She knew Mary's pacing, and her ashen face when Bob was travelling. She was not alone. Bianca was sleeping soundly, as five-year-olds do. Catherine couldn't quite fathom why Mary spoke of her child then, her great love.

Catherine called Harry and then curled up on the couch. Mary brought her two pillows and a comforter, smiling now, a weak smile. She wanted to give Catherine something, but Catherine shrugged her off. Mary began to cry softly. "I wish I could get a grip," she said. Catherine did try to understand, but she sometimes felt irritated until she saw Mary tremble, pacing again.

It was a few years later when Catherine understood completely and felt ashamed. She had been impatient, hard. Even when she had given into Mary's irrational fears, she had resented her weakness, barely covering up her contempt. But then she was left alone when Harry died. She kept her chin up, and smiled when everybody showed genuine feeling for her. She kept busy straightening out papers and objects, some to keep, some to toss. She was proud that she was able to handle her loss, even when Lila went back to school.

One night she stepped onto her balcony and looked at the sky. The moon was just a crescent. There was silence. Everybody was asleep. She suddenly felt a pang of helplessness. She was completely alone. She was afraid, and then she was panicky. Where could she go? She went inside, reeling a little, clinging to the sofa. Mary's face came back to her, pleading, apologetic, trying so hard to be understood. Catherine then felt every shudder Mary had suffered in her insecurity that she might not have the strength to overcome her fear—a child, the greatest demand of one's life in her frightened hands.

It was 12:30. It was much too late to call somebody. She got a book. She stacked up the pillows on her bed and climbed in, covering up, feeling cold when it was not cold. She pushed the book aside because she could not read. Time passed. Minutes were hours.

At six o'clock she called Mary. "Please come."

"I'm on my way."

Vindication

Ivan had a pair of eights. "Gimme three. I'll get ya," he said. He picked up a jack, a seven and a two. Even bluffing wouldn't work. He threw the cards into the chips on the table and stood up. "Go to hell, friggin' jerks. I'm leavin'." He had been complaining all evening about his cards. When Rolf McGrath told him to pay up, Ivan swept the chips and cards off the table and left the tavern.

A hefty man, unkempt, but not bad-looking with a strong physique and piercing blue eyes, Ivan beamed with pleasure when he was referred to as Ivan the Terrible, not knowing the history of such a person, but liking the sound. In his thirty-five years he had not given thought to improving his personality, and only circumstance had kept him out of serious trouble.

Ivan had inherited land from his father, a harsh, combative man with an inappropriately high intellect who had scooped up property in Northern Michigan at every opportunity, and was overseeing a handsome spread. Jacob Webber had leased land to farmers for many years. After Jacob's death in 1961, Ivan, his sole survivor, figured that the income was sufficient. He had no interest in taking care of the land. He took a job for ready cash with Neustadt Delivery Company, a trucking service that transported farm products and equipment throughout the Upper Peninsula, to satisfy his hunger for gambling, women, and beer.

He had married and fathered two children with a plain, heavyset woman who had cleaned the office of his employer. Hilda Bergmann, at thirty-one, had never married, and hadn't expected to be fulfilled in motherhood, although she had held a deep longing for children. She knew that she did not look very attractive. Her pleasant personality was admired by thoughtful people, but she was easily overlooked by most men. Ivan had shown a little interest in her, making remarks about her body, and although Hilda was embarrassed by his crude remarks, she did not ignore him. She was flattered when Ivan asked her out for a beer, and, after a few such meetings, he suggested that they live together. Ivan knew that women in general were not interested in him for other than short motel visits, and he wasn't doing well with pickups at Feeney's Bar, where he was a regular with losers and dissolute women. Hilda was an easy target.

With misgivings, driven by loneliness, Hilda had consented to his offer. Her only request from Ivan was that they marry before children arrived. "You ain't goin' nowhere without me, woman," he said. "Get that straight right now, but if you want that sort of shit, I'll go along. Just don't expect nothin' else."

The family lived in the suburban hamlet of Oak Hill, within the reaches of the rugged but beautiful Lake Michigan State Park. Ivan's old farmhouse was in a deplorable state when Hilda moved in, and she had cleaned it to the bare floors. She scrubbed the kitchen and bathroom fixtures, which were neglected and filthy, and she worked with whatever she could find to make a home. Ivan tossed beer cans, cigarette butts and dirty clothing wherever he happened to be, but Hilda shrugged off his thoughtlessness and picked up after him, resigned.

She had kept her old Toyota, so she was able to drive into town, eighteen miles away. Ivan didn't give her any money, but he had accounts in most places. Everybody knew Hilda and didn't question anything she asked for. She even purchased supplies and tended to a rich and productive vegetable garden. On occasion she would gain some cash just by being shrewd. Poker nights were every Saturday night at Feeney's Bar, and Ivan played regularly with men of his caliber. It was an opportunity for Hilda when he came home bruised and disheveled, falling into bed exhausted from brawls. When he tossed money around and forgot it, Hilda left small coins scattered, but socked away most of the money in a hidden mustard tin.

Her babies had arrived within just two years of the marriage, to Hilda's delight. The children, Paul, eleven now, and Freda, nine, were fine children, lovingly and wisely cared for by their mother. Paul was the more sensitive of the two, often too insecure to speak his mind. Freda was a wise little girl, ahead of her peers. She read everything she could get her hands on. Both children loved schoolwork, and the teachers had particularly high regard for them and their mother, knowing the tightly-controlled lives they lived. Hilda had told the staff that she had simply made it clear to her children that the pathway out of hardship or need was through schools. She knew that a few years down the line Ivan would declare destructive demands for the children, particularly Paul. He had already stated that he would take Paul out of school when he was strong enough to join the work force. His mother was building up a determined resolve to counteract him.

Hilda did not pursue contact with her neighbors. Small town paranoia held her back; her husband's sociopathic personality was well known. Even the farmers avoided his bluster and ignorance. Hilda accepted the situation, considering herself sufficiently blessed with her two children. Nor did the children have close friends. Word got around that the Webbers were outsiders. But the brother-sister closeness was profound and protective, and Paul and Freda were inseparable, each showing deep, demonstrative love for their mother. They always took the time to help with the housework—and the garden—determined to lighten the burdens their mother was always eager to carry for them.

Fortunately, the neighbours always had a friendly wave for Hilda, and the women sometimes arrived at her door when Ivan was noticeably absent. They had casseroles that "just happened to be too much for the family," and cakes and cookies "from experimental new recipes" that Hilda's kids might enjoy. A neighbor from a large farmhouse that Hilda admired from her back porch gave her a Tommy Hilfiger jacket for Paul, and a lovely cashmere pullover for Freda that her daughter had grown out of. Francine Sommer, a popular science teacher, gave Freda a fake fur dressing gown for her mother. "Don't you dare tell your mother that it got too small for me," she told Freda with a big smile. "Tell her it shrank in the washer." They enjoyed a laugh, and Ms. Sommer felt a tug at her heart when she watched Freda walk away clutching the plastic grocery bag Ms. Sommer had used to disguise the gift.

The gifts caused a little embarrassment for a while, but there came a time when Hilda felt proud enough to accept the gifts without apology. Her proficiency with needlework was outstanding, and Hilda donated magnificent place mats and towels and scarves to town charities and school fundraisers, made from fabric remnants. They were snapped up at such events. The seasonal affairs awaited Hilda's donations with special anticipation. Hilda attended a few affairs, but was noticeably uncomfortable and shy. Everybody welcomed her with open arms when she was emboldened enough to attend, but they did not try to persuade her to stay, knowing her circumstances. She was also unnerved about being away from home. Ivan had locked her out a few times just to show his malice. Had it not been for the children, she would have had to plead with him to let her in.

When their father was at home the children concentrated on their homework and a little television, saying very little. Family life was on edge when Ivan was home. He was not as powerful as he pretended to be, but his lack of any trace of compassion was a mental burden.

A terrible experience had exacerbated that permanent pall over the household when the children were advancing in their studies and growing more self-assured, an event that left Hilda and the children defensive. Ivan was reaching for a beer in the refrigerator when the refrigerator door struck Hilda's arm. She was pouring water from a steaming pot into the sink when the boiling water hit her left hand. She screamed in pain, and Ivan, immediately annoyed, brought his arm around and struck her across the face. She fell to the floor as the children ran to her. In agony, she couldn't control a deep moan. Ivan stared, grunted, and moved away.

Freda and Paul helped their mother to a sofa in the living room and covered her with a quilt. She writhed in pain. Freda, with her sharp intelligence, had taught herself many aspects of personal care, aware of the possibilities of harm within the home. She wrapped a cool cloth around her mother's hand and fetched two Tylenol pills from a cabinet. Paul was crying pitifully, so Freda hustled her brother into the kitchen. "I'll take care of her," she said to Paul. "She'd feel better if we didn't make a fuss. Serve up the supper. Let's get that over with." After holding her arm around her mother, soothing her and waiting for the pills to take effect, Freda brought a pillow and a blanket to the floor beside the sofa, preparing to spend the night beside her mother.

Paul set the table, even setting out a meal for his father. He and his sister sat down without the heart to call him. He arrived, however, said nothing, ate the food and left, taking another beer from the refrigerator.

The winter of '74 was dragging, and the summer kitchen was waiting for the replenishment of venison, goose and chicken. Hilda's hand was healing well with the determined care of her daughter. She put on heavy gloves and dug up dark earth and stared at the sky. It was still early, but the land was loosening up, even with slowly melting snow. Ivan had taken up with a woman in a neighboring town. Hilda took advantage of his absence to encourage the children with their schoolwork and to prepare for a fruitful spring.

When he was on the job, Ivan often travelled far, leaving Hilda alone with the children. Hilda, of course, preferred the long trips, at which time he would be gone for several days. She was free to pour all her time into enjoying her children, and she cherished the opportunities. The children were ignored by their father when he was at home, so she made a point of having fun with them. In winter they spent a lot of time outdoors, every inch heavily padded from the cold, and Hilda helped them build forts. And they built snowmen, and they sledded and made angels in the snow. In spring she pushed them in a wheelbarrow into the lush grasses and dumped them while they squealed with delight. She planned two swings with strong ropes, one on each side of an old oak tree. Paul beamed with joy as he shinnied up the tree to get the ropes in place, and he helped his mother saw up an old log to make seats. All three tugged on the ropes to make knots, by no means professional knots, but brilliantly strong. They all giggled about "swings for two so nobody would have to swing alone." On hot days in summer Hilda took the children to a pond near the woods, allowing them to strip to brief underwear to take cooling dips.

Self-deprecating, Hilda often gazed at the children with pure joy, wondering how their beautiful, smooth skin and fine features came about. She tried very hard to be attractive to them, and dressed with care, kept her hair clean and shiny, and often put on a little makeup. She knew that the children loved her very much. She needed nothing more.

The children devised a pact with their mother. When their father was in town and spent the evening gambling and drinking, they knew that he would be dangerous when he arrived home late. Hilda was forcefully told to waken them at the approach of his car, if they were not already awake, and all would go quickly to the kitchen. Hilda would hold them close to her, one on each side. They would defy him without saying a word. He could not beat all three of them, and he was nonplussed to see the little wall of three, ready for anything he had to give. After shouting and throwing things about, he would then shuffle off. On the other hand, when he came home unexpectedly he would display his macho image at once, pushing Hilda, demanding her presence in the bedroom, forcing himself on her for hours. Hilda often whimpered, but remained stoic, loathing the fact that the children in the nearby rooms were able to hear every movement.

As the months passed, Hilda knew that Ivan was planning to make his demand soon on his growing son; he told Paul to talk to the teachers and see if there were requests in the area for workers to do manual labor. Hilda had several teachers ready to back her up and confront Ivan as best they could. There was another fear, unfortunately, that was also worrying Hilda. Ivan was taking long, hard looks at Freda and her developing body. He began muttering words, "fleshy, firm, ready," while looking her up and down. He openly told her brother that he should remember "what girls are here for." The comment left Hilda sickened, but Freda remained composed and quiet, feeling poorly concealed contempt for her father.

September arrived with cooler weather almost immediately after Labor Day. School had begun again, and Hilda avoided any mention of it in Ivan's presence. With the change in the weather there came wolves. They howled nightly. Hilda didn't expect them to threaten the children during daylight hours when she and the children stayed close to home, but everyone was uneasy knowing that they were in the area. When Hilda drove to town she also noted headlines in the local papers which reported sightings of black bears, warning parents to watch for them. A large male was particularly aggressive and had been scared off with flares and gunshots to hold him at bay. In most instances, of course, Ivan was not at home, so Hilda kept the children close to her and kept her fear deep inside. "Wolves and bears are cowards," she told the children. "They only come around when it's dark and we're locked up and safe." She smiled gamely as she spoke. The school bus driver thoughtfully arranged to pick up the children and drop them off at their very door when the wolves and bears were about.

Hilda knew that Ivan's pitch to get Paul out of school was irritating him, and he was planning to show his son who was boss. It was a cold night with a driving rain when he told Paul to go to the garden and pick up some cabbage and carrots. He wanted to sell them to a friend. He kicked a bushel basket toward Paul, who stared at his father, his face drained. Hilda immediately said that it was too dark, and the wolves were close. Ivan pitched forward, pushed her against the wall and held her by the throat while he bellowed, "Keep out of this, stupid bitch. That kid of mine has to become a man, and he'd better get his fuckin' butt outta here right now. Get movin', kid, and don't come back without a full load."

Hilda collected herself, her face strained, and stepped toward Paul. "I'll go with you, honey," she said.

Ivan grabbed her arm and pulled her back. "Like hell you will," he said. "Move it, kid."

Paul grabbed a wool jacket and hurried to the door with the basket, expecting a blow any minute. Freda moved directly to the outdoor light switch and turned it on, staring at her father with defiance. Hilda gripped the counter, terrified.

Paul returned with the basket heavy with greens and carrots and mud, his saturated body shuddering from the cold and fear. His face was gray as he tried not to cry, but he fell into a corner and began to sob. Ivan made a move toward him, but Freda ran to Paul and stood in front of him, screaming at her father, "Leave him alone. I'll KILL you if you touch him." Her pale little face was twisted with hate, and she was in a state neither of her parents had ever seen. Her voice was rasping, animal-like. Ivan stared at his daughter, unexpectedly stunned, his mouth open, and then he laughed, a weak, guttural laugh, and left the room.

Hilda, knowing that Paul would be beaten if she had interfered, held back. Had she had a weapon she would have used it. Next time she would be ready. A little later she slipped quietly into the garage and found an eight-inch knife with a strong steel handle. She put it in a drawer close to where she prepared food, and closed the drawer. Freda watched her mother and said nothing.

Strain from the endless need to protect her children was becoming evident in Hilda's face. Freda watched her mother closely, and she fought back tears when she noticed that her mother was getting a noticeable tremor. That evening Freda told Paul that she had a plan.

The first weeks of October were fickle, sometimes sunny, but more often there was a cold rain. However, the winds began to change with the shorter days, and they soon brought scattered snow. Paul tended to a lively fireplace without being asked. He tried very hard to please his father so that he would not be singled out—or even noticed. Freda continued to study with little effort, often reading some of her English compositions to her mother, and Paul talked about electronic things that were inscrutable to his mother. She reveled in their bright dialogues, flushed with pride.

It was Saturday, poker night. After consuming large quantities of roast chicken and several beers, Ivan noted to anybody that happened to be there that he was going to "get Percy that night and stuff him into the toilet." There was a piercing wind when he left in his pickup and headed onto the unpaved artery that branched off the main road to the town, cutting off a few miles.

About three miles into the wilderness Ivan's pickup suddenly lurched to the left and hurtled down a steep, rocky hill toward a swamp. Ivan stood on the brake pedal, frantically twisting the pickup right and left, but it did not stop until the front wheels were deeply entrenched in the bog. The windshield had hit a heavy branch and was shattered. Ivan leaned back for a few minutes to get his bearings, his heart pounding. He pushed the door open and stepped out, his boots sinking into thick mud, his neck feeling a strong whiplash. The pickup had lost power. He was not close to any habitation. He groped around the cargo bed for a shovel, trying to reject the fear that his situation was hopeless. There was no shovel. He moved back into the cab, out of the wind. He pulled his leather jacket close, hoping to sleep, but he was too cold and too tense, and the wind rattled the sides of the cargo bed. Glass was scattered. The glove compartment held a few matches, but no candles.

Ivan decided to walk to keep his blood flowing and to seek help somewhere. He stepped out clumsily, the mud heavy on his boots. His feet were numb and unfeeling for a few steps. Just at that moment a shadow crossed the rugged terrain, and then another. Ivan stopped, his breath heaving, and looked around. In the faint light from the snow-covered ground he saw wolves to his right and left. He backed up, feeling for the door of the pickup, and reached for his rifle behind the seat. It was not there. He quickly moved back inside. The wolves paced around the pickup, and claws were scrambling for purchase on the side of the metal door.

The wolves suddenly scattered into the woods. The pale light from the window of the cab became dark.

Aunt Trudy

"Steph, leave it alone. Now!"

Steph was fascinated by the lovely scarf wrapped in tissue, and she wanted to touch it. Her aunt had just purchased several new items from St. Petersburg, and the scarf looked soft and silky. Aunt Trudy had brought the items to show Steph's mom her "divine new duds." Steph had always wanted to be like her Aunt Trudy with her long blond hair. And Aunt Trudy dressed in clothes that Steph saw in magazines and on TV, keeping up with all the fashions: the short, tight skirts; the fabrics that wrapped around her and made her beautiful; the sweaters that were wool that didn't itch; and high heels that were so skinny that Steph wondered how they didn't break, even though Aunt Trudy was quite small.

"Go and comb your hair, Steph, and pick up those magazines. There's always such a lot of clutter in this room. I don't know how your mother stands it. She's no housekeeper, that's for sure." Steph's mother, stacking dishes in the kitchen nearby, heard the remarks but ignored them completely.

Steph moved away again, disappointed. She wanted to be near Aunt Trudy, and she often told her how beautiful she was. Even at twelve

Steph felt fat and ugly with her dark school clothes and jeans and flat shoes. And she didn't know why her aunt always rejected her. Every time Aunt Trudy came to visit, Steph would run to her and put her arms around her, hoping she'd be glad, but Aunt Trudy always brushed her aside with remarks that would hurt a little, such as "Please, Steph, you're too heavy to be so pushy," or "Really, Miss Clumsy, watch it."

Aunt Trudy criticized Steph's mom also: "Margaret, your hair! Even if you don't want decent color, all that gray stuff could be helped if you'd see a real hairdresser." At one time she even told her sister to bend a little and buy something that didn't come from Walmart. With Mom's cheerful disposition and sense of fun she generally ignored Trudy's remarks, or she would just laugh. One time she told Trudy with a big smile that her new shirt was from a shop she had just discovered— The Salvation Army. Everybody laughed, but Steph knew that it happened to be true. Her mother didn't make excuses for anything.

The two sisters, only a year apart, couldn't have been more different.

At the dinner table later with Trudy, Mom and Dad, and her brother Jimmy, Steph was enraptured as usual when Aunt Trudy told everybody that she would soon be off to Europe. She said she needed some time away from the dull people she worked with. She always came out at the top of high end sales in the prestigious Wood Thrush Real Estate firm. She knew exactly how to greet new prospects, being aggressive, but with a flirtatious humor that worked every time. "The other agents, especially the men, have a hard time, even with their own listings," she had said, "and they expect me to do everything they can't do themselves. I've made it on my own, and they don't like my success," she said, and she called them "wimps and mama's boys." They couldn't even read the Stock Market like she could—with a little help from a friend here and there.

When Aunt Trudy talked like that, Mom was not particularly impressed, and she once said that surely all the guys knew that it wasn't just her great salesmanship that brought her success. Aunt Trudy just sneered, and Steph didn't understand what her mother meant. Dad was always quiet when Trudy was visiting, and when she was not there he called her a narcissistic sociopath. Mom would just smile and say, "Perhaps." Steph didn't understand that either. She was quite sure it meant that Aunt Trudy didn't like other people very much. Maybe she was too smart.

"Oh, by the way," Trudy began again, "I'm buying a new house."

Mom said, "Oh, Trude, where? But your house is fantastic. Why?"

"Why not? I tell the people at the office that it's because all the closets are full in my place and I need bigger closets. The truth is that I'm sick of the neighbors where I am. They're jealous, and they don't like me. Some of them have kids, and they're noisy brats. The new place is near the causeway at Chokoloskee, but still on the mainland, at the edge of the Glades."

"I've seen that development," Mom said. "Those are big places. They'd be too secluded for me. All I can see around there is dirt roads and Spanish moss."

"So? Like I said, kids are noisy, and Bernard will be with me when he isn't travelling." (Steph had learned that Bernard was a friend that Aunt Trudy "hung out with.") Trudy continued: "All the lots have to be two acres, so what's not to like? Besides, I like one house in particular that's well on its way. Some people can't see why I'd want to be in the boonies, but I don't see it that way. The privacy will be terrific!"

"Will you still come to visit your peasant family?" Margaret asked.

"Knock it off, Margaret. I'm not going to live counting nickels while I can help it."

The school year was finishing, and Jimmy just passed his courses without distinction. Jimmy was a jock. Steph did very well with her marks, excelling in science and math. Dad always praised her for that because, as he said, the future is already demanding those subjects, and the humanities are almost out of the picture now. Mom always agreed with that, but deplored the fact. She said once: "You may be right, Jack, but machines will never bring us artists and writers of great books. What will become of history and fabulous museums when people don't care? It seems like natural beauty won't matter either because everybody will be staring at stupid screens. I see lots of people at the malls walking like zombies because they're staring at their I-pads, or whatever the heck they are. And all the pretty natural places are being chopped up for housing. How about our very own Everglades? Soon we won't even recognize them with idiots bringing in more weird animals."

Aunt Trudy came in the following weekend with her new house plans. It wasn't as big as Steph had imagined, but it would be beautiful. There was an area on the main floor for a small bedroom and bathroom for Helena, Trudy's maid, whenever she was needed overnight. Trudy stressed that fact more than she talked of the four upper bedrooms and square footage of the house which were more than she would ever need, even for her big parties. There was a very large "theater" room planned with a few steps up which would beg for plush carpets and seating. The front entrance was lovely, with large double doors and two elegant pillars that were just the right size. A double garage was on the curving driveway at the side of the house. Trudy always scoffed at people in general who built homes with huge garages in front. "That makes the house itself look like an afterthought," she stated. The entire main floor was raised, as many in Florida are because of the ever-present dampness. There was no basement. Trudy hated basements. They were "cat-challs, mostly for junk."

At the end of September Trudy's furniture was moved into Number Four Starlight Drive. Building had continued while she was in Europe.

The workers welcomed the jobs eagerly, so the home was almost complete, with a few details in progress at the exact time that had been promised.

There was a very large van chugging into the property when Steph ran in to see her aunt and to rave about the house. Trudy even had a bit of a smile when she told Steph to take off her shoes. "That floor is solid maple, Kiddo," she said.

Aunt Trudy had already had window treatments put in with yards of diaphanous white silk. There was an aura of pale blush, not-quite-pink pastel throughout the lower level. Aunt Trudy called the wall color in the living room "Candied Mist," and adjoining rooms a closely related "Palest Tulip." The thirty-foot "theater" room was paneled with walnut. A library or den was a little lighter, as was all the trim and molding, in what Trudy called a toasted maple. The atmosphere throughout was, to Steph, pure elegance. Her face shone with admiration for her lovely aunt who somehow never seemed to warm up to people and yet had such good taste.

The front of the property was not yet fully landscaped. Several red bud trees had been planted, and numerous azaleas would be outstanding in the spring. Gardeners had been there, clipping and pruning the natural trees and bushes, but they had been given strict orders from Trudy. She wanted the growth to be wild and plentiful; she didn't want "prying eyes gaping in her windows."

To Steph's delight there was a small stream at the furthest point of the backyard. There were dragonflies, and small minnows darted at the edges of the water.

Steph's mother asked Trudy with a trace of sarcasm whether she would be having a housewarming party, but Trudy just laughed. "No way," she said. "Bernard is staying for a while at first, but I want a quiet, private place to call my own. Parties later when I'm ready and everything is ship-shape."

Bernard left for Dubai for a few weeks with some colleagues when Trudy had settled in. She didn't know what his meetings were about and didn't care. "He would just bore me if he talked about his work," she had told everybody.

September had been rainy, but detail work was still on schedule, and the October changes in the trees and skies were gentle and beautiful. A slight breeze made the leaves flutter, and it was just about seventy degrees when the gardeners were putting in new grass in the backyard. Stretched out on a cushioned bamboo chaise longue, Trudy was enjoying her spacious patio, and she watched the men as they watched her. She wore a brightly printed sarong with a big white hat. She sipped a Tom Collins. She knew she looked alluring, but she also knew that she was safe with the men working steadily. They had been told earlier that they were taking too many breaks and the work was falling behind. It wasn't, but Trudy had to let them know that she was a taskmaster.

There were small jobs to be done inside, but when the men needed to be there Trudy took off for the malls. Her private papers and documents, as well as fine silver and exotic ornaments, were still locked up in bank vaults, where they had been placed for the transition. There was a screen door that had a faulty latch and didn't close properly. The expensive door was of foreign manufacture, and the new lock system had to be ordered. Two tiles also had hairline cracks, and Trudy insisted that the entire foyer be replaced.

Steph had hoped to impress Aunt Trudy when Halloween was approaching. "I'm staying home to give out candy," she said. "I'm too old to collect candy." An art class project had been the designing of Halloween costumes, but Steph didn't tell her aunt because Aunt Trudy had said Halloween was stupid for everybody, not just kids. "Dumb costumes and grubbing for sweet stuff. The people are just asking for rotten teeth with all that crap."

In the late afternoon of Halloween Trudy stopped by her sister's house to give her some blankets she was going to toss until Margaret said, "Toss them my way. I could use them." Trudy was riding in a white Jaguar with another man, and she briefly explained on the run that she was tired of Bernard's trips and was just seeing this guy to fill in. "Introductions later, Marg. It's Howard Goss. We're off to dinner. I'm not going to be around for the little vultures looking for handouts."

The children had left the dark streets when the couple returned to Trudy's home. She had left only a front light on, and Helena had gone home early to spend the night with her children. The couple sat on the patio for a little while, listening to the sounds of the night. An owl sounded, and Trudy said, "I don't like that sound. Owls are creepy."

"I like them," Howard ventured. "I hear an owl responding. Nice."

"Yeah, speaking of night life," Trudy said, "We're going to have to move in soon. The bugs are getting to me. Those mosquito traps don't do much, do they? By the way, what's with the drinks? I'm dry."

"I should go. I've got a lot of explaining to do, especially after last night," Howard said. "Millie knows something is up."

"C'mon, Howie, live it up. Stay." She sauntered up to him and pulled him out of his comfortable chair. "Get us some more drinks."

Howard Goss left at two A.M. They both had been drinking non-stop, and he was thick-headed when he slipped out the door, wavering, and drove away. Trudy was sound asleep.

There was no sound when the door began opening very slowly. There was still no sound when Trudy felt a pull on her right arm. She tried to turn over and realized that she couldn't.

"Howie?"

There was still no sound. She tried to pull herself up and found, but could not see in the dark, that something was pinning her down. She screamed, but still couldn't move her arm, or part of her torso now.

Her legs flailed, and then she realized that her breathing was strained. She was gasping. She pulled again and found that she had lost most of her strength. She had to stop struggling.

When Steph got home from school the following afternoon, her mother met her at the door, keys in hand. "Steph, honey, take the keys to Aunt Trudy's house and run over on your bike," she said. "She isn't answering her phone, and she told me she was going to let Helena have the day off. She was supposed to be home all day." Steph was only too anxious to see what the home looked like now.

Steph's young life became deeply tarnished forever. When she stumbled out of Aunt Trudy's front door screaming and collapsed on the sidewalk, a passing driver had seen her and backed up quickly. Steph saw only a black curtain, and she vaguely remembered trying to go back to sleep because there was something there that she didn't want to accept. She knew she was being put on a stretcher, and the voices she heard seemed to be deep within a well. Flashing lights were everywhere. In the maelstrom of her tortured mind thoughts whirled, and they were cruel thoughts that seemed to stab her heart. Her vision returned to Sunday school, where she learned that the serpent was the symbol of evil and chaos. She also saw a figure which she had always found terrifying, dismissing its true meaning: a serpent eating its tail, representing the cyclic renewal of life, death and rebirth. She tried to sit up then, with gentle hands trying to soothe her, and she began screaming "No, no, no!" The only words that were clear to her were *Burmese python*.

Ya Think?

(A Story Told by a Teenaged Girl)

I was getting ready for bed upstairs when I heard snow crunching. I stopped to listen. Who could be at the back door on such a night? My heart started pounding. I turned off the light to get a good look out my window. It was bright outside. There was no moon, but the snow was everywhere. I couldn't see anybody. But someone could be on the porch. Under the porch roof below me.

Dad was working late over in Jantzen County. He's a lineman boss. He had been asked to gather his crew for a power outage. Mom was still downstairs waiting for him. She was doing her needlework in the kitchen near the warm Franklin stove.

I grabbed my terry robe to run downstairs when I heard my mother shout. I made the stairs in a couple of leaps, and she met me in the hall. "A man was staring at me in the back door window," she said. Her face was drained. I grabbed her arm and pulled her under the stairway in the hall. "I heard him," I said. "What will we do? Is everything locked up?" I asked Mom if he had tried to open the door, but she was too stunned to have noticed.

In my hurry I had left my iPhone upstairs. "Stupid me," I thought. The land line was right in view of the kitchen window. I was too scared, and I had to get a grip. I used all my inner stuff to get my mind working. I grabbed Mom again by the arm. "C'mon upstairs. I have to get my phone, and I want you to lock yourself in the bathroom."

Mom pulled back. Her eyes were wide. "No way. I'm not going to leave you by yourself," she said. "Maybe we're safer upstairs, but I'm not leaving you by yourself," she said again.

"No, Mom, please. I need to think." She wouldn't listen. I thought then that a fifteen-year-old daughter is not the best person to protect her mother in a scary situation. If only Dad or Kevin were here!

While we were running up the stairs, Mom continued: "We're safer as two, but we should find a weapon."

I snatched the phone from my bookshelf and hit 911. There was the usual stupid *"If this is an emergency, press 1,"* but they said they were on their way when I sputtered out our address. Brother Kevin was off at University, and Dad was too far away to get back, but Uncle Brian lived in town. I woke him up, but he was right on the ball. He said immediately, "I'm on my way. You can hack it, honey. He may go away, but get something in the kitchen." He probably, like, meant a knife, but heck no, neither of us wanted to go near the kitchen again.

"Just hurry," I said. "The police are on their way, but please hurry."

I had recently skimmed over a newspaper item. A man had entered two homes within a week. A mother in one case had been raped and beaten and left for dead while her children were sleeping upstairs. She managed to crawl to a phone with a broken jaw and a deep concussion after gaining consciousness an hour later. Not far away from there, two gals in an apartment building had bravely used andirons to fight off a man after their door had been left unlocked. The violence had brought neighbors running, and the man had leaped a railing and vanished into the woods. I was, like, too spooked. I didn't finish reading the article. But I remembered that the poor mom was so deeply traumatized she could only say that he smelled of leather and grease, and he was strong. Their town was across the canal, and I guess I considered it a bit too far away to worry about. Now the article came back and hit me. I tried to shake it off, but it made my fear worse, even if this wasn't that creep.

I was thinking mostly of my mother. I had to protect her. I felt weak. I was mad at myself 'cause I didn't have the courage just to be calm and face the guy. I don't know what I would've done if I had seen that man's face. I think I probably would've passed out. I was in a situation that showed me to be, like, a healthy, young, silly coward. I thought if the man got in somehow, I'd just run.

My thoughts went to the windows. Maybe the man felt that smashing glass would alert neighbors. Our old house had storm windows, and they were in place. Dad had seen that they had to be sealed tight with the severe weather we were having. Winter had come early; late October had brought in harsh winds and snow that didn't let up much. Way too early, I thought. I now liked our old, well-constructed house of brick and mortar and small windows. They seemed to be better protection, especially now.

As a family, we had often discussed firearms in the home and the heavy-handed NRA. It seemed to become something of an understanding that we would not keep them. We talked of the high percentage of horrible gun crimes that happen within the very homes of individuals. It became somewhat of a referendum with us that they would not be in our house. We didn't think it was worth it. Even our Kevin would never have hunting equipment. He was an avid nature lover, tough and strong, a champion of the forest, but totally against the destruction of wildlife. He had no reason whatsoever, he said, to kill animals, and made no excuses.

Now, however, I wondered what I would do if I had a gun. I would be unable to handle it, and it would probably be in the wrong place at the wrong time. Oh well. The thinking vanished and my thoughts came back to the present.

We were in Kevin's room looking for "something heavy" when I thought of his camping gear. He had a machete for clearing brush. When I pulled it from the closet shelf, I saw Mom move back. It grossed me out too, but, like, self-preservation is the strongest force known to man. I figured I wouldn't use the horrible weapon, but I felt kinda safe holding its sinister handle.

We made a point of being quiet a bit to listen. Could he have left? We stood by the bathroom door, ready to bolt inside. In fact, I placed the machete inside the door to fight back if we had to.

The wait was probably less than ten minutes, but seemed like an hour. "Mom, stay here. That will be the police or Uncle Brian," I said, when I heard a car screech into the driveway. "I insist. You'll be in the way. I'll come back soon."

Uncle Brian arrived just behind the police. He slammed his car door and ran to me at the open door. He put his arms around me and said, "I've heard of this punk. I think he's just a peeping Tom, but I'd sure like to get my hands on him." He was avoiding his real thoughts. "Becky...your Mom's okay? Upstairs?" I nodded.

A policeman and a policewoman hurried in after Uncle Brian and locked the door behind them. Everybody shook hands fast while the policeman was speaking. "Fred Chamberlain here, miss. We don't want to waste any time. Show us the window. We'll scour the neighborhood." Uncle Brian motioned to them, and they headed toward the back door, Uncle Brian leading the way. "Lock the door behind us," he said. "I've got a key. Keep calm. We'll get him."

"Yeh, keep calm like. Fat chance," I thought.

When they were going out I noted that they had to unlock the dead bolt, and I felt a chill wondering what would have happened if it hadn't been locked. I locked it again and dashed away. The door still felt creepy. I didn't like being near it. I raced back upstairs.

Mom seemed calm now. The police gave her security. She was more relaxed than I was. We listened to low voices as the three circled around the house. Then we went to my bedroom window and saw that they had fanned out in a large area of the field, poking at footprints and heading to the trees beyond.

"I'm going to go down and make some coffee for them," Mom said then. Her color was back to its pretty glow. I knew she wouldn't let them go without offering something.

The three of 'em came back disappointed. Tracking had been difficult. Children had been playing in several spots that day, and a lot of tracks were hard to make out in the crusty snow. The police officers and Brian graciously refused the coffee. "I have to get back, Becky," Brian said. "I have to be on the road at six-thirty. Look at the time. It's almost two." The police also wanted to get back to plan the next move with the intruder. They would return in daylight. They gave Mom and me strict instructions about the doors and windows. They also did a rough search of our house. They circled the downstairs area and showed a little impatience when they saw that there was a motion detector that flooded the back property. It had not been activated. "Don't leave that off for as much as a second at night," Officer Chamberlain said. "We're going to drive around the neighborhood for a bit when we leave," he added, handing me a business card. "Call at any time whatsoever."

Mom and I went upstairs right away. It felt further away from the danger than the lower level. I left the machete at the top of the stairs, actually feeling a little security with its hideous presence.

After we had restlessly settled into our beds, there was a sound. I had no idea what it would be. It was just a sound that didn't feel like my imagination. I knew it wasn't my imagination when Mom came to my door, frightened again. We stood rather stupidly wondering where the noise had come from. We thought it was near the front veranda. I took the first step down the stairway and Mom stayed beside me. I gently urged her to move back, reaching for the machete. She grabbed my arm but I shook her off.

I sorta felt him before I saw him. The front door was open and I immediately noticed a small pane of glass missing as I saw him, a large man with a sneer. He was wearing a dirty suede jacket and a fur hat with earflaps. He held a gun, casually swinging it back and forth. "This door was easy," he said, sounding like an animal growling. "They didn't look in the van down the street. They're not protecting you now. I knew two dames were alone here tonight."

He swaggered closer, glaring at Mom. She was cringing, terrified, and began to plead with him to leave us alone. It was at this point that I finally got a grip. I was transformed. An unknown spirit within me gave me extreme power. The machete sliced through the air, and my aim was fantastic. It hit his upper body with a great thud. The sharpest part slammed into his left carotid. His eyes gaped, his gun fell, and then he fell.

I wasn't losing it after all. I ran to find Mr. Chamberlain's business card and called him back. I was sitting on a low step holding Mom when both officers came back. There were heavy gasps when they saw the man and a lot of blood. They were speechless.

Maybe I was just being a smartass kid, but I had to say it:

"I beat you to it."

Sampson Quarry

I.

June 2007

Nobody locked doors in Sampson Quarry. The townspeople enjoyed the cliché. It was one of the givens that kept people living in the town, proud of being there.

"We're all so close," Frances Storey said, smiling and opening her arms in a sweeping gesture. "Lily lives across the street, and the Olmsteads are right on the other side of my driveway. The fields are wide open, and there just isn't any place to hide. Fortunately, we also seem very happy being stay-at-home domestic engineers, as they say." Everybody smiled. Frances was a typical homebody. She was raising four children, and had gained too much weight from a daily routine of childcare, soap operas, and afternoon snacks. Her opinions often echoed the television dramas that were all she cared to know. She wasn't aware of much in the way of human rights or climate change or politics, except to often declare what a "real strong conservative" she was.

Helen Diedrick, a statuesque five foot eight, agreed with Frances. "If some idiot thinks he won't be seen trying to rob a place," she continued, "he'd have a hard time with us neighbors ganging up on him. We're always aware of anyone or anything strange in our town, and if people find the place too small and too boring they should just move." Her emphatic remarks brought the usual colour to her face. She had the ultra-blonde characteristic of pale, porcelain-like skin that became flushed when she was emotional, and her high cheek-bones were prominent against her bright lipstick. "I think we'd all think twice if we were in a big city where they have to have bars on the windows and dead bolt locks everywhere. What part of the country is nicer than our part of Ohio?"

"Imelda doesn't go out at night at Michigan State after dark, even with the campus bristling with police," Betty Branson from the end of the block added, chuckling, always managing to bring her daughter who was "off the charts" into the conversations. "She doesn't even trust the campus police!"

The women were part of an audience at a five-household garage sale and cookout, and they all had set smiles, agreeing and nodding wholeheartedly. The sales were going well on the long tables, and baskets of the smaller items were nearing empty. White elephants changed hands readily, and everybody was in good spirits. In the morning there had been a question about the weather, but it had held. The clouds drifted away and left a mild breeze and sunshine. Perfect.

"I'm looking forward to the guys getting home, Betty added. "Fred ordered the ground beef set up in patties, and they're 'B-I-G,' he tells me." Everybody enjoyed the day, and some of the fun had been caught on Frank Lopez's cellphone just one week before the murder took place.

John Halliday had been in his open garage checking under the hood of his new Toyota when somebody entered just after dark and attacked him. He most likely didn't even see his assailant before he was struck. Nobody had seen or heard anything until later on that evening when his wife, Rochelle, went to see what he was doing. The head wound proved fatal the next day at Memorial Hospital. John had not gained consciousness.

The town was in tumult. John had been known as a quiet, salt-of-the-earth husband and father, but most of the shock displayed an affront to the perfect order of the town. How could this happen on a quiet spring night when most people were watching television or putting the kids to bed? It seemed that a phantom had sprung up from nowhere and perpetrated an unspeakable crime in an idyllic place of virtuous citizens.

A red car. Little Cathy McEwan kept talking about a red car. Her big brown eyes were wide, hoping somebody would listen, but a six-year-old wasn't expected to grasp the gravity of the hideous crime. Everybody was frantically talking at once, vocal about footprints that should have been found but were not, and much thought was given to delivery persons from other places. Hadn't anybody seen a man who was not a local? The killer couldn't have been a woman considering the intensity of the physical attack on John. Apparently the instrument had been a piece of concrete.

Police cars and yellow tape and media trucks soon dominated the scene. And the police did not have any compunction about knocking on doors and scrutinizing homes, questioning every person. Everybody understood and accepted them. All the locks and safety measures were snapped up at the hardware store. Guns were added to the already well-stocked homes, and Sampson Quarry became an armed camp.

John Halliday's funeral brought an emotional crowd that poured out of the church and went directly back to locked-up and now securely alarmed homes. The bereaved Mrs. Halliday was never left alone. Her oldest son prolonged a stay from school in Michigan to help her cope and to prop up his teenaged brother. Prepared food was delivered without fanfare from the neighbors, much more than Rochelle Halliday would have ordinarily had in her kitchen.

Cathy McEwan was eating her cereal before catching the school bus a few days later, when she told her mother that she saw the man. Her mother was arranging lunch in her backpack when she stopped short. "What man, honey?" she said. JoAnne had suddenly felt a cold chill; she immediately sensed that something important had been overlooked. Cathy said it was the man everybody was talking about. Her mother sat down beside her. "Cathy, tell me, what do you mean?" she said. She remembered her daughter talking about a red car and nobody had listened to her in the initial fear and horror of the murder. JoAnne now very intently listened to her daughter.

JoAnne waved the school bus driver off and called Tony to come home. She called Betty Branson and Angie Olmstead, the more level-headed of her friends. The four adults hovered over the bright little girl, and listened—finally.

Cathy began: "Billy lost his baseball before Mr. Halliday was hurt, and we ran to look for it in the lane behind Billy's backyard, behind Billy's garage. There was a big man there that told us to beat it. He wouldn't let us look in the grass, and he started to come to us. We ran. He was standing by a shiny red car. He looked really scary, real big."

"Folks, we're wasting time," Tony McEwan said abruptly. They knew then what they had to do. Two police officers, Rob Delaney and Stan Field, arrived within minutes. When they talked to Cathy, they were instinctively gentle, and the neighbors that had begun to crowd into the McEwans' house were politely asked to leave. Cathy was staying close to her mother, a little shaken up now with the direct questioning, but she was glad to talk to them now that they were listening. Rob Delaney put Cathy at ease by suggesting that they would love a cup of coffee if she or her mother would make some. Everybody smiled when JoAnne hastened to the kitchen, and then he said, "Cathy, you can help us. Let's slow down here." Looking at JoAnne, he then said to her and Cathy, "Do you want to talk to us about it now, or shall we come back later without our uniforms and police cars and stuff?"

Cathy told them she was okay, so they sat with mugs of coffee and talked to Cathy about her school work and the teachers, etc., before any further prodding. Officer Field left through the front door and ordered the media crew further down the street.

The little girl was so precocious that she surprised the adults. "All the mothers and fathers talk about how safe we are and we don't get scared of things, and when Billy and I saw the man we knew he didn't live here, but we didn't tell our parents because our parents don't hear us, but we were scared of him. When we heard about Mr. Halliday, Billy and I both thought it was him that did it."

A few days later the officers asked Billy's parents if they could talk to Billy. The parents, Glenda and Foster Wilson, were reluctant. They were a shy, reclusive family, generally smiling at neighbours, but rarely mixing. However, knowing that they were a part of the upheaval that had visited their neighborhood, they consented, pointing out that they would be in attendance with any interviews. And their older son Benjamin was to be included in any discussions.

They both stood behind their sons and gently held their shoulders when Billy was being questioned. Billy was petrified. Officer Delaney was accompanied by Sergeant McGrange, a super-upbeat man with a friendly smile and a profoundly ethical pride in his work. The officers were very professional in their understanding of a closely knit family, and tried to keep them calm. "Billy, would you know the man again if you saw him?" Sergeant McGrange said, pushing aside a notepad and pencil, smiling directly into Billy's face. "You young guys often see what older folks don't. We often think we're too busy to notice things we should see."

Billy couldn't smile, but he spoke clearly and seriously. "I remember that he had a big body and a lot of hair," Billy said, "and he looked really mad at us. We were scared. If I saw him again I think I'd know him, but I don't know for sure." When he was asked what kind of car it might be, Billy said it was "just a red car."

"You're right to be careful about strange people," Sergeant McGrange said. "You never know what they're going to do. We're thankful that we have some smart kids in the neighborhood to help us."

The men prepared to leave after noting a few pertinent questions about telephone numbers, email addresses, etc., Sergeant McGrange asked the Fosters if Billy would be available any other time he might be needed. The Fosters nodded in agreement, still hovering over their sons. "Is that okay, Billy?" he said directly. Billy nodded.

Tire tracks in the rarely used, overgrown lane suggested a GM car with Michelin tires. Footprints were not conclusive because of deep grass. A small paper on the ground, torn from a pad, had a smudged address written on it. It was found to be the penciled address of the only service station in town, Bertrand Auto. A check at the service station of that name came up with nothing. Fingerprints were illegible. It could have been dropped by anybody. Nobody remembered a red car with a big man unknown in town.

The Sampson Banner, the local newspaper, announced the sighting the children had witnessed, along with a sketch of what a possible car would look like. The newsfolk had discussed the reporting at length, some believing it was the wrong thing to tip off the owner. Others believed overwhelmingly that the word should get around so the community would be aware and vigilant. A sketch of the man, drawn with Cathy helping, was also shown. It was not convincing, but the children had been frightened by him and had retreated, knowing only that he was big, and had a beard. A dark-haired man with wild hair and a beard and big shoulders was all they created. One of the editors said, "Better than nothing."

So it was that only two very young members of the community held any possible knowledge of what had become a terrible crime in a confident neighborhood. Every adult in every conversation was stymied. Nothing whatsoever had been seen or heard. They closed up their homes and stayed inside as soon as the sun went down. The investigators kept the children in their sights while they talked to everybody in the town. Cathy and Billy had been told to let their parents know if they remembered anything besides the few features of the man they had seen. The townspeople became introverted and uneasy, even while moving about in the neighborhood by day. A police van became a fixture in the lane where the children saw the man. The media vehicles thinned out, but kept some equipment in a field close to the main center of a small strip mall that was the business and shopping area of Sampson Quarry.

II.

Days became weeks with not a scintilla of evidence to work on, and police departments throughout a large range of the county had gathered with residents, hoping for someone who knew something tangible to decipher from a brazen crime. Even footprints in the garage showed only the Hallidays'. It seemed unreasonable that other footprints were not found. Checking into records from John Halliday's life and work showed a man who played by the rules. It was with total frustration that every person involved with investigative work kept records of John's cruel murder close at hand.

Businesses and educational facilities moved on as usual. There were not many teenagers in town, and they had to be bussed to Weyland, a school fifteen miles away for all grades from seven to twelve. Weyland High was actually highly regarded as one of the finer secondary schools of the county. The young people were respected, and most of them had ambitions for higher education and making a mark. There were, however, a few somewhat indulged teens who were allowed to run after hours, particularly on weekends. They hung out near the quarry that gave the town its name.

Sampson had been an early settler on farmland, and he was a shrewd farmer who purchased land in the area at every opportunity, eventually breeding prize cattle. He raised a large family with the help of a demure, stay-at-home bride, and he brought many people who had coveted his success to the area. The town grew, but in the eighties most people had become "yuppies," looking for greener pastures, so the town of Sampson Quarry remained static, small and self-important. Those who had come earlier, had seen, and had conquered the town, liking it just the way it was. There was a typical old post office and newspaper office. A kitchen products light manufacturing building hired many on their way up the ladder, and insurance companies somehow banded together, enjoying traditional inhabitants of the town, some adding tax work for the people. There was a hardware store that handled a great variety of goods that brought people into town, and a few ladies' wear shops. Enjoying a few eateries, the more conservative types hailed the fact that there was only one bar.

The teenagers had wiener roasts and pot parties at the quarry, which had a shallow pool in its center, rocky and rough below, but refreshing on hot summer days for the kids nimble enough to swim and enjoy the rugged surroundings.

It was these teenagers that found a hopeful clue for the police. It was six weeks after the crime, a warm, early summer twilight surrounding them, that Josh French and Marsha Cleary wandered off from their friends at the quarry and found the car. It was in a ravine, partially submerged in brackish ground water, almost invisible because of its state. It had been burned and blackened, probably pushed into the muddy ground water while still burning. In the darkening sky Josh and Marsha saw that only a hulk remained, with a few shards of glass and a thin body part showing shiny red metal. Marsha said immediately, "It's the car! It's the car the kids saw. It has to be!" Josh was puzzling over it at first, but soon recognized what Marsha was saying.

"Oh my God! You're right." They fled back to the gang, Josh shouting, "We found the car! C'mon. Take a look."

Their friends stared initially, wondering what car they saw. Then it hit them, and the entire group ran to the site. They all got a good look at the trashed metal, but with instinctive wisdom they did not touch anything. Josh French got his phone out first and called 911.

The headlines on the Sampson Banner screamed on the evening delivery the next day: CAR FOUND. POLICE INVESTIGATING.

After a thorough search of the site where the car was found, tape and small flags were placed, with a No Trespassing sign. The hulk was driven through town later on a flatbed to Bertrand's Garage. Many people watched from their homes, feeling a little creepy. There were several police officers at the garage, and the trashed car was driven into a shed which had been cleared of all car parts and equipment. Around-the-clock surveillance was planned. Town and county officials came in groups, examining the remains of a late-model car. Serial numbers had been hacked out, and the car had been doused from top to bottom with extremely flammable gasoline. Its total destruction made everybody think that a second burning had been made through a second visit to the wreck. The tires were shreds, and the top and all the inner seating were nonexistent. Somebody exclaimed rather vividly that it looked like a pile of melted black glue.

Again, frustration held sway with the search for a clue to the provenance of the car. Under scrutiny, and with little to go on, it appeared that no sedan of that size or shape had come off the recent assembly line anywhere near Sampson Quarry. Two pieces of red metal, burned, chipped and faded, and a few nuts and bolts, were all that could be detected in a search for clues to a horrible murder.

III.

Summertime, usually a time of pure joy for Sampson Quarry, was blighted by the crime. Time passed with no new leads. Everybody sadly suspected that it would become a cold case, a miserable remembrance of a good man. And the town, too, showed a quite distinct change in attitude. There seemed to be a loss of pride. Rochelle Halliday had left town. She had told everybody that she had to get away for a few weeks, but she had wired her house to the nth degree inside and out.

In September a circus came to town. It was a small affair. No tigers. No trapeze artists. But there were exciting rides and funny clowns and booths for games, etc. The circus had visited Sampson Quarry before, but this year it was a quieter, more sober attraction. Everybody vowed not to disappoint the children, so the show was well-attended. However, the children, even the teenagers, were given orders that couldn't be questioned. They were to stay with adults every minute, and under no circumstances would they be able to leave the grounds without their parents.

The McEwans each held Cathy by the hand as they pushed through the crowd. She was eager to ride the Ferris wheel, and even though JoAnne and Tony didn't have the faintest desire to ride, they decided to go with Cathy sitting between them. Cathy beamed. They were heading for the big wheel in the noisy crowd when Cathy suddenly pulled backward and shouted, "It's him. It's him!" her face white, her eyes wide.

Tony and JoAnne stared ahead, and the people around them stopped abruptly. There was a strange man staring at the highest point of the Ferris wheel. At first the noisy crowd drowned out Cathy's scream, but when the people suddenly stopped to stare, the man turned toward them, and before the people could get their bearings he was gone. Tony pushed Cathy into JoAnne's arms and took off with a group of men who had instantly followed their instincts to run the man down. They headed into the only clear path to the fields that surrounded the circus, leaving a stunned group of people wondering what to do. Some were quizzical, but others knew exactly what was happening.

JoAnne and Cathy went home with a large group of neighbors, everybody in a state of fear, clinging to each other psychologically, one voice breaking the ice by saying, "They say there's safety in numbers." One could feel distinctly the disappointment and rising apprehension when everybody realized that the man was still in the area. His rapid flight also seemed to confirm the fact that he could have been the killer. There was fear also about the safety of the men who trailed him.

The men arrived back at Tony's house two hours later, dejected, and described what had happened. The man had slipped away. He obviously knew a way through the pine trees at the edge of the parade grounds that held the circus tents and rides. This time footprints were evident, and the men called the police. They had waited until the police arrived with night goggles, a bloodhound, and light standards, keeping the crowds away from the footprints. A specialized security team was prepared to spend the night. In a very short time it was obvious that the police response was exemplary.

JoAnne hugged Cathy. "Honey, you were amazing. You described that horrible person just like he was, and you remembered," her mother said. "He had a big beard, and he is a big man, isn't he?" Everybody who had been aware of the sighting agreed. Cathy showed fear for the first time since her initial sight of the man. She clung to her mother. JoAnn spoke then: "Hey, gang, please stay for a while. I'm going up with Cathy to get her to bed, and I want to continue to talk. Don't go away. I'm coming down to get us drinks, or make coffee, or whatever." Everybody agreed. She returned to a thoughtful group trying to find some hope to cling to.

"Damn it!" JoAnn said. "They have to get some action on this crime. All of us are getting miserable, and the children don't deserve to be scared all the time. It rubs off on them when we can't hold back our own fear and anger. Apparently the schoolkids don't go to the quarry any more. Whether we like it or not, we're prisoners of that bastard."

Everybody agreed. "JoAnn, I couldn't agree with you more, but what can we do?"

Frances Storey said. "Surely something will break. Maybe the footprints will get us somewhere, but they seem weak. He'd dump the shoes."

So the neighbors all tucked in the kids with special care that night, and the doors and windows were locked tight. Some of the families had even placed bars earlier on their lower windows.

The bloodhound had followed the tracks to a sluggish stream that led into the quarry. It had lost the scent there. Apparently the man intentionally fled through knee-deep water to cover the scent. The footprints on the ground showed size 14 Ked sneakers. Casts were made, and the police directed bulletins within two hundred miles to all dealers in Ked footwear, accompanied by the little they had regarding pictures and the general description of the man. The tracking evidence was displayed across the country.

Detective Alan Davies was optimistic after the sighting. It was irrational to think that anything solid had been learned by the appearance of the man, but he said openly to a squad of police getting ready for a drill, "Look, guys, we have to think of this event at the circus with fresh minds. He is still around. He must have a reason. It's a lot better than wondering if he has skipped town forever, leaving us with no hope. Let's try it that way. We will find that bastard, and we will start today." There was a murmur of agreement.

District Investigative personnel called several town meetings in the following weeks at the town hall with everybody asked to attend. Several people from neighboring towns drove in, eager to help or at least support the local people. One man, Charles Jessup, from the small town of Sunnyvale, spoke up immediately after introductions had been made.

"I saw the man at the circus. I was one of the gang that took off after him. I have been looking back, and I wonder if anyone has considered the crowd at the Ferris wheel. Who was he looking at? He was looking straight up. Do you think he was looking at someone in particular?"

The crowd was momentarily silent, and then they became animated, questioning each other. One could hear "I hadn't thought of that," and "He must have been looking at somebody," etc.

The police chief thanked Mr. Jessup, and said that the fact had been mentioned, but only as a question of why he was standing still and looking upward, and then the thought had passed. Then he spoke to the crowd: "The gentleman here has raised a good question. We have not pursued that idea. What do you think, all of you? We could talk to the Ferris wheel operator." There was a "Yes" from many voices. Mr. Jessup continued: "It seems a long shot, but I think it would be something to consider. He had some interest in the big wheel, didn't he? Of course the area was crowded, and there was a lineup for the Ferris wheel, but what the hell, let's try." Everybody clapped, and the police chief thanked Mr. Jessup. "I think you have given us a possibility to investigate, Sir, and we thank you. God knows we need all the help we can get. Perhaps we should have followed up earlier on that thought."

An older woman stood up and spoke: "Officer, I think you have done everything in your power to help us. This is a very difficult crime, if you ask me. You look for footprints that should be there and are not, and you have only the words of two bright little children to go on. We adults seem to be useless so far, so you have our blessings to keep doing what you're doing. Thank you!" There was a cheer from the group.

The Sampson Banner printed the results of the latest town meeting, and almost before the ink was dry a call came in to the Sampson Quarry Police Headquarters. A young man's voice clearly stated that he had used his cell phone to take pictures from the Ferris wheel. He and his girlfriend were there at approximately the time that the sighting took place. He said he'd be happy to show his pictures. All the folks on duty were elated.

The young man was gangly, dark-skinned, and neatly dressed in a brown leather jacket. The police took to him right away. His name was Neil Rodriguez, and he was from the neighboring town of Tamarack. He spoke in a tone which was intense, no-nonsense, and direct. "We were up high when the people were still getting on down below. I don't like heights, but my girlfriend was enjoying the panoramic view all around the circus grounds. I took pictures from high up and also while the Ferris wheel was going around."

After a cursory run of the film, and before they scrutinized it closely, they decided to get every head together to share the viewing. Everybody on duty and off arrived within an hour, and word got around. Residents began to stream into Town Hall as equipment was being set up, eager to hear any news revealing any possible clues to go on. Neil and the officials were excited and eager after the quick showing had revealed some very clear movements from the circus grounds. The Hall, as usual, was packed to the doorways. Cathy's parents had been asked to join the officials that were hoping for more input from Cathy, who had become something of a very young heroine. However, Cathy was being closely watched by a neighbor at home. Her parents had decided to leave her at home. She had had too much attention, and she was becoming close to tears from her own anxiety.

The mayor, Gerald Emerson, was on hand, and he shook Neil's hand with a firm grip. "I'm hopeful, Neil. We have had a hard time with our loss of a good friend, and we haven't had much to go on. Let's hope you found something for us."

The young man followed the group to the stage. The crowd greeted the mayor and his entourage with applause, but clapped louder and shouted when they saw Neil. He moved to the front of the hall and stood beside the people on the stage. A large screen dominated the room. Nobody knew what to expect. Neil was asked to talk to the crowd.

Happy to oblige, Neil spoke: "I was with my girlfriend at the circus, and we decided to take a ride on the Ferris wheel. I had never been on one before, and I wasn't too keen on it, but my girlfriend Sandra wanted to see what it was like way up high. I took pictures with my iPhone looking around. There was a lineup, and we all got on slowly, so I knew we'd have to wait before going around. I got some views of the people down below getting on after we did."

When the film began, the large auditorium was silent. The moving picture showed girders and black sky, bounced around, and then closed in on people wandering down below. Almost immediately Detective Joe Fiona shrieked. The viewers on the stage moved close together, watching, frozen to the spot. The man was in the picture, down below. There was no mistaking his large stature, the beard, and thick hair tied in a ponytail at the back. He was giving tickets to the Ferris wheel operator, and a young couple moved into the swinging chair just as the film changed to some people in the line behind him, then a panorama of the crowd. The film continued, but showed only laughing people on the way around the circle. The audience in the town hall was standing, some with tears, some jumping up and down. There was a long way to go before the people would have their grips on the man, but this very clear, fortunate view of a possible murderer was a break in a long, dry case that had left an entire town in upheaval. The suspect obviously had reason to stay in town.

The Police Chief spoke to the crowd, many of whom had been caught up in the excitement without having clearly seen the subject or his vision on the screen. "Folks, I think we have something to go on. This film will be scrutinized with a fine-toothed comb, and our Cathy McEwan will be our guide to finding this man." Some people chuckled at the thought of a sharp little six-year-old child advising the police force.

The Ferris wheel operator remembered the man, but with indifference. Only the large beard and stature of the man were unusual. He had taken the man's tickets for a young couple that was belted into the seat, not giving much thought to the man's appearance in a very diverse crowd. He shrugged when he was asked if he could recognize the man or the couple in any way. "Maybe." Invalidated tickets had been tossed away.

The crowd dispersed, and the police huddled with Neil. They decided to keep the plans quiet. The neighborhood knew, of course, that a good lead was finally giving them hope, but the pursuit of a young couple had to be followed up without giving them a chance to change appearances. The search would be difficult with only a distant view of a young couple that looked like everybody else.

IV.

The students went back to school, and cold weather moved into Sampson Quarry. There was a noticeable change in the season which was abrupt. Halloween was subdued; the children were eager to dress up and get their treats as before, but they were more than happy to have several adults on the streets with them. Thanksgiving was the same. Warmth and friendliness were still characteristic of the town, and students arrived home for the holidays from many parts. There was a difference, however, even when time had given the townspeople a necessary need to move on.

Rochelle Halliday appeared on occasion, not as often as before with John, but she always received genuine welcomes and offers to help her with anything at all. She seemed to have shouldered her burdens well and always refused help.

Fred Branson put their feelings into words one Saturday night at a cocktail party: "We've lost a little of the pride we had," he said. "Maybe we used to be a little cocky. Nothing could mess up our great town—no crime, no fear, no thinking twice about asking a neighbor for a trip to the plaza. We've been trifled with, and even though we have recovered most of our respect and ease with each other, a mark is still an undercurrent in our every thought. If the crime had been solved, we may have felt better, but the crime is still part of us." Everybody agreed with Fred, but it was generally accepted that the town would never be the same, and that was a real pity.

The families decked out the houses with abandon at the beginning of December, determined to "be cheerful" for Christmas. The weather was wintry with wind and cold, but there had not been a great deal of snow.

Two weeks before Christmas some of the members of the Sampson Quarry police detachment were preparing to call it a day, after working overtime as part of the Specialized Surveillance Team. Detective Joe Fiona and his crew had had a quiet evening, with just a few telephone calls about heat deprivation and a few family squabbles from everybody drinking too much. Talk was sufficient with the police men and women listening and giving advice to calm things down. As some were collecting coats and scarves to head home, a loud knock sounded at the front entrance. Everybody froze for a moment, and then hurried to the door. Helen Diedrich was standing outside the glass door, wide-eyed and frightened. Several hands reached for the door. "Mrs. Diedrich, come in, come in. What's the matter? What happened?"

"I'm so sorry," Helen exclaimed. "I have to talk to you right away. It's about the murder."

Some stood rigid, others moving closer. Officers down the hall had come running as well. Rob Delaney led Helen to a chair and sat her down facing a group of eager faces. "Helen, I'll get you a cup of coffee—or whatever." a policewoman said. "Do you want something stronger?"

"No," Helen said, "I have to get back. Jerry's uptight. He wanted to come with me, but somebody had to stay with the kids. I didn't want to make a phone call that could be overheard, and I wanted to keep this thing away from the kids. I saw that man at the mall, and I don't understand it at all. He was with Mrs. Halliday. When I caught sight of her I was on my way to greet her when I stopped in my tracks. She was in the Food Court, which was packed, and I saw her before she saw me. She was talking to that man. He gave her a brief wave and then left her. They both looked serious. I got stuck in traffic both ways, and was sorry I even went so far to Warburg County. It was worse on the way home or I'd have been here earlier." Her audience was gaping, stunned.

"I told Jerry about it on my way home. I sort of thought I shouldn't use the phone somehow. Do you think it was alright?" Helen was on the edge of her seat, blurting out her words. The entire station was spellbound.

"You did the best you could," Joe Fiona said. "You're brave to hold it in. As long as nobody heard you. You will have to keep your phone safe; as a matter of fact, may we have it to hear your conversation fresh and new?"

"Of course," Helen said, groping in her handbag. "I should have called you from the mall. I'm so dumb. I kept thinking somebody would overhear me. I was in shock."

Nobody was going home that evening. Helen Diedrich was taken to a comfortable room where a Keurig coffee pot and various mugs were sitting on a long table, partially cleaned and tidy. Two big chairs and two sofas faced each other. Rob Delaney called Jerry and told him everything was under control. They would be sure that Helen got home safely. Jerry had to be a part of it. "What do you think of all this?" he said. "I can't believe it."

Rob agreed. "Join the club," he said. "We'll be in touch."

The first words from the officers were to be expected: "Are you SURE it was Mrs. Halliday?" Also: "Are you sure it was that man?"

"I'm sure," Helen said. "I saw that man at the circus. His beard was shorter, but the pony tail was the same. He has a big face, easy to spot. I hope all of you realize that I'm more than positive that I saw him, and her too." Helen was looking around at wide-eyed faces in shock. "I'm in near disbelief myself, folks, and I wish I hadn't seen them, but I did."

A near chorus spoke then: "We believe you." All were puzzled, minds racing, ready to start a new day late in the evening. Helen was noticeably tired from the questioning and from her own traumatic experience, so the group suggested that she get home and get some sleep. She would be needed big time as the discussions progressed.

V.

Alan Davies was a burly, white-haired no-nonsense man, highly regarded for his ethics. He had a slight limp which did little to damage his erect and powerful carriage. He had retired the year before the murder, and returned to duty by request, although his return was a necessity to him. He had been a proud lawkeeper in the town of Sampson Quarry for forty years. Much of his character was reflected in the good feelings and contentment of his townspeople. His voice was commanding; one knew that he had nothing to hide and expected nothing less from others. His limp had been nobody's fault. He had come upon black ice on an incline close to town a few years earlier, and his leg had been badly broken when his car hit a concrete abutment at uncontrolled speed.

Davies and his group took places at a long table the next day, planning what the first moves should be in the situation now gripping all of them. Detective Inspector Al Brophy had arrived early to join them, and had been poring over documents and papers connected to the crime. He moved into the group and immediately began:

"I mean no criticism of any of you in this situation when I say that all of us—eight I now see around this table—should not know about this sighting. With Mrs. Diedrich and her husband and all of us that's too many for the privacy we are going to need in the plans to go ahead. A slip from anybody's lips could reveal a case wide open with a probable perpetrator in our very neighborhood. I don't know how to stress the necessity of secrecy." Everybody nodded and accepted the reality of danger.

Carol McCullough, a bright trainee, spoke up: "I think we all see this as a fact," she said, looking around. "I feel burdened by the very knowledge of what Helen Dietrich said. She should have come to only one of us—probably you, Detective Brophy, but she was overwhelmed and eager to tell us. We trust each other, but can we trust ourselves? Helen had the smarts enough to know that she shouldn't tell her children, but had to surely tell her husband."

"Right you are. I talked to her this morning before anybody was up after the night of no end. What time did all of you get to bed? I heard it was about four."

Carol stated that she got to bed about four but didn't sleep at all and should have just stayed up.

"Helen is meeting me at the library after one to get caught up," Al added. "She said that she and Jerry will not tell a soul, and I somehow think they'll pull it off. I trust both of them. Helen said she regretted not taking a picture of the two of them with her cell, but they were just splitting up and she was in shock. She thought she should get lost in the crowd. There's no doubt that she could have been caught taking the picture as well. I think she did everything right."

"Let's get to work, folks," Alan Davies said then. "We'll have to plan surveillance and see what's up, and we have to fade into the woodwork while we're doing it. First of all, we need to get ordinary, well-used, insignificant transportation and start watching her movements. We don't need to have our friggin' uniform everywhere we go either. I will be in bomber jacket and jeans and a baseball hat when I'm not on duty. We can't let anything slip.

"Are we ready?" Detective Al Brophy said finally. Chairs scraped back in unison, and the entire group was on a real high, determined to pursue a final and unbelievably important break that was going to take their every talent.

"One more thing," Alan Davies said, "We have to see very little of Helen in the open. She stated that herself. She suggested that it would be a good idea if she kept away from the station. That's why we're meeting at the library—in the Raleigh Room—just by chance, supposedly. Every small incident could be watched, like her visit last night. We had better not pressure her; she has told us everything she could possibly tell about her interrupted Christmas shopping, but she wants to help us figure this out. Can't blame her. What a shock she must have had."

"And now here's the hard part," he continued. "Our appearances are fairly well known around town. We have to do more than just run plain cars with street clothes. If we watch her or trail her, we can't let her know. We have to pull cops from other locations—strangers to the people here, but chosen carefully. That Bob Reese over in Tamarack runs a tight ship. And we could use more women; somehow they aren't watched as much as men." Subtle smiles followed, but all agreed.

The following Wednesday at 8:00 A.M. was called for a confidential meeting with all pertinent police personnel on hand. Detective Inspector Al Brophy called on Officers Rob Delaney and Stan Field to "get on the blower" and coordinate the central dispatch area, and the detective surveillance team had to drop everything and get this "bloody thing together."

Brophy stressed timing. "We are not going to lose any time here. No partying for the duration. We are going to do our professions proud. No friggin' fooling around. Get some sleep, folks. We will be one great surprise for the bastards that killed John."

VI.

A specialized surveillance team was handpicked, all eager faces willing and able. For the beginning of the night surveillance, Rob Delaney and Stan Field were assigned to a spot parallel with Rochelle's front yard, but half a mile away. State of the art camera and binocular equipment was clearly disguised. They were driving a regular gray van. Stan was unshaven, a well-worn leather jacket on his well-built torso. His untidy countenance was changed considerably. He had always been a natty dresser.

Dense fir trees blocked the view of Rochelle's front facade, but the driveway was clearly seen. Their parked van was just one of many vehicles, and there was a steady stream of holiday traffic passing them in each direction in and out of town. They would move from time to time, still within the busy traffic area. They were in close radio contact with two young police trainees in a building behind the Hallidays' backyard. A surprisingly convenient, unused barn-like warehouse had been found, quite well stationed for watching Rochelle's back entrance. The neglected windows had to be washed simply for acceptable vision. The day shift moved into the same assigned spots. A minivan was replaced with a black sedan, and the back view was good, even lighted well by two close lamp posts.

Surveillance had begun. Police personnel were on twenty-four-hour duty on all arteries near Rochelle's house. There would not be a time when she would escape notice.

Rochelle was an early riser. She was often on the road by 8:30, just for marketing. She also spent a lot of time at a coffee shop in the mall close to Rob and Stan's assigned parking spot, reading magazines and using her Smartphone. At one point a new car was seen in her driveway; it turned out to be her youngest son's Nissan. He rarely stayed long, and seemed to be just dropping in after work. He worked in an insurance office in town.

Two detectives from the neighboring town of Sunnyvale were assigned to seek out Rochelle's personal records, search warrants at the ready. The bank held the big secret of the woman everybody was eager to know about. She had $750,000 dollars in Mutual Funds, and a couple of savings accounts in other six figures. Deposits were made twice a month in amounts close to $10,000 each, all in her name only. Activity on the accounts was to the date.

Rochelle's telephone access was tapped, and her Smartphone was always in her hand. She talked about library books and meetings of a Book Club. She ordered sheets on sale by Internet. She asked about a black coat at the dry cleaning shop everybody knew. There was nothing unusual in any word she uttered. It was six days before anything out of the ordinary was noted. She headed out in the evening of the sixth day toward Warburg County. All points were alert. She would be followed at a safe distance, and after Selig Street a new driver would merge in, letting the other disappear. Several other officers at the station were eager to get going. A half dozen other policemen and women had volunteered from adjoining towns to take part. New faces and bright personalities were like predators trailing a deer.

It was quite immediate that the newly developed surveillance was worthy of the plan. Actually, two cars lost Rochelle temporarily. She took an obviously circuitous route, even driving through a lane with access for only one car. A plain-clothes officer from a small hamlet close to Sampson Quarry circled around the block and picked her up half a mile ahead after she emerged from the lane.

Rochelle drove to the county line at a busy three-artery crossroad and turned into a sprawling garage complex with scrapped cars to the left and several transport trucks lined along the treeline to the right. Rob and Stan followed two cars behind hers, radios in close contact with the officer, wide, dark glasses and sheepskin hats shielding their faces. As Rochelle veered to the left, Rob and Stan headed to the right. The other policeman moved in and moved to a tire pressure air pump.

The wide garage windows were revealing, to the delight of the stalkers, with just advertisements for motor oil and retreads, etc. Large letters on a white frieze above said Gillebrand's Full-Service

Gas, Body Shop & Supplies. Behind the counter, a black man with sideburns was accepting cash for a large, rolled-up floor mat. He waved at Rochelle as she made her way to a table piled with magazines. A large man with a beard was moving into a back room with a small group of men. Rod's heart skipped a beat. Could it be? Too soon. They had to get a better look.

It was hastily arranged between the police cars that a pert, black female police officer, Diane Miller from neighboring Valeria, would enter and ask for a tire gauge. She was told to take in as much as she could, and was given a brief description of a tire gauge. She picked up the plan immediately. She headed toward the front door of the garage with a matter-of-fact gait that was perfect. She spoke to the salesman behind the counter, saying she was about to purchase a used Chrysler with big tires and someone had suggested she purchase a tire gauge, among other things, and keep a tool box on hand. She and the salesman had a warm chat about it, and she had the personality to make it work. She said she didn't know anything about tires except that they rotated when she was driving.

She walked to the table where Rochelle was sitting and rifled through the magazines, speaking directly to Rochelle: "Is the latest *Time* magazine here? I missed it this week, and I have to straighten out this miserable world, so I need to know what's happening." The two women smiled freely. "Me too," Rochelle responded. "These are mostly motor mags, unfortunately."

"Yeh, I guess," Diane said, and left the garage, tire gauge in hand.

When she hopped into her car the coterie of police hunters in all vehicles snatched at their phones and waited for her to talk. She was wisely aware of the new situation, however. She started: "Listen, guys, I think we shouldn't expect too much. We have to get back to the shop and sort things out—the location, particularly, don't you think? I'm glad I will recognize her up close now, but I have done nothing. I can only report that she had a yellow pad on her lap and a white bill or something with the letterhead *Bertrand Auto Parts*. She knows me now, and I should be outta here!"

Diane was right, of course. She, her partner and two officers in a car close by headed back to Sampson Quarry. Rob and Stan stayed. After doing a good surveillance of the cars and transports, they moved out of the parking lot and drove around the block. It was a dark access road, and at the far reaches of the back of the station it was densely wooded. "We have to go in," Stan said. "I think we'll have to walk. Can we get these wheels into a good spot?" At a grove of trees they turned the van, crossing a shallow ditch and appreciating four-wheel drive. They drove over snarls and heavy roots, happy that the area was obviously rarely inhabited. They were well out of view of the road when they left the van and began to push their bodies through the dense brush. "I know poison ivy in the daytime, but in this light we're taking our chances," Rob said with a humorous snicker.

They managed to lumber through the growth, watching every step in the darkness. A dog barked some distance away, to their dismay, but they were nearing the back of the station. At close range they saw a fence, barbed wire eight feet up. The fence was shrouded with heavy growth, almost impossible to see. They moved in and Rob carefully pushed aside some greenery, taking care not to touch the fence. A faint hum from a gate to the right made it likely that it was wired. He got a good look in the direction of the service station.

Rob spoke in an undertone: "It may be...oh, my God!" He didn't go further with the sentence when he saw stacks of burlap bags underneath a rough covering of tarpaulin. On the deep slope to the left there were sheared-off stalks of cannabis. He knew it well. The high fence extended several yards further, high stalks of marijuana growing in profusion. "Let's get out of here. Let's get back ASAP with this."

Before they trudged back, they took photographs. "This is too easy," Stan said on their way back. "If that's where they hang out, we have to get back and start working. I can't believe our good luck! Do you suppose we found their operation? Is this the reason for the murder of a decent man? It seems too easy."

Some cars stayed near the station after telephone contact. Others hurried back to the Police Headquarters, radios contacting nonstop. As they were leaving, a silver van had pulled into the parking lot, a large black woman at the wheel. It moved to the far left of the darkest part of the lot. After a short delay, the lights went out, and the woman looked in every direction before slumping down in the very dark cab of the van. A rusty pickup crept into the lot from the adjoining field and stopped behind the wrecks, out of view, almost impossible to be seen. The engine stopped. Two men edged down, faces obscured by dark hoodies.

At Sampson Quarry headquarters the personnel on duty were not eager to go home. There was simply too much to take in, and the excitement was overpowering. Everything was happening too fast. At the peak of their discussions about the next moves a call came in from Eugenia in the silver van: "Listen," she said. "A black van just moved into the lot and parked at the front door. It's blocking the front entrance for me. New York plates. I'm taking pictures, and something about it makes me feel we're on to something. I think I'll get out of here before they suspect me, and, by God, I'm cold!"

Alan Davies had been in Headquarters all day. He had received a call from a young man in Ridgefield, about fifty miles away, and he was elated. "Yes, Eugenia, get back here now." he said. Rob and Stan are punching in too. I think you knew they were in their own van, right?"

"Sure did," Eugenia said. "See you soon."

Two officers from neighboring Tamarack were more than alert, concealed behind broken car parts. They zeroed in on the van. *Superior Force Car Parts* was a splashy sign within a rising sun logo on the sides. Two men had left it idling as they went inside. Several people inside the shop moved toward them as they went in, including Rochelle Halliday. She hugged one of the men and led him into the back room where the small group had entered earlier.

Detective Davies emerged from his office with an unusually animated look on his face, a look that made everybody look up. "What are we doing?" he said. "I'm afraid somebody is going to get hurt. Let's get this show on the road. This job is a murder scene, and the liaison between Rochelle Halliday and what has to be her accomplice should be snatched out from under them. I want to take a big chance. Let's wait until the folks report back, and then let's get everybody in our force, and the guys and gals in Tamarack and Valeria and Sunnyvale. I've just received some fantastic information that we'll talk about later. So far the excellent leads got us only crap results until now, and these bastards have to be brought in. We might be taking a big chance, but we've found the source, and a surprise friend in way off Ridgefield just set the table for us in no uncertain terms. Let's plan a cleanup without wasting any more time."

A meeting was called for 7:00 A.M. the following morning. Staff Sergeants and District Inspectors and all available personnel were to be on hand at the Marriott, forty miles away from Sampson Quarry. Security would be of the essence. Only then would everybody learn about the "fantastic information" Inspector Davies had.

The following evening at dusk the operation began. Rochelle had been within eye shot of police personnel since her discovery at the garage. She had not returned to Sampson Quarry. She had left the garage a couple of times with a few others, including the man who was now fairly well established as the bushy-haired killer of her husband. They entered a sports bar for the most part for a few hours, but went back to the garage, often carrying pizza or other takeaways. There obviously were sleeping quarters for several employees behind the showroom. The police personnel had taken shifts, changing vehicles where they were obvious.

Rochelle had been in attendance at the garage throughout the day, often waiting on customers, and it appeared that her partner was in the back rooms. The police moved in from several directions, planned as several minutes apart, on standby in parking lots along the way, and on side streets, and in the back sections of used car lots, etc. They were closing in.

At what they had termed "the witching hour," a rather unremarkable 9:30, they moved in. Two detectives from the town of Sunnyvale, man and woman, went into the shop, smiled at Rochelle behind the counter, and wandered over to the tire section, casually examining the new snow tires on display. A hatchback and a sedan were parked, quietly waiting behind the wreckage, and Ron and Stan were behind the now-disabled electric fence. A minivan and two sedans entered the front parking area, the minivan circling the lot past the transports, stopping at the back entrance. The sedans were parked directly in front of the building and the drivers each got out.

Detectives Bob Reese and Joe Fiona pushed through the door, in full uniform, guns drawn. They shouted, "Don't move one inch! Get to the floor! NOW!"

Five faces stared, momentarily stunned. Then a man reached toward the lower counter, screeched, and fell back, his left arm hit by a bullet. The detective pair circled around, guns pointed at four people who were dropping to the floor.

Very close to the same second, the back entrance had been entered the same way. Rob and Stan, in uniform now, shot the heavy lock system on the back door, moved in, and stunned four people. Rochelle Halliday stared, ghostly white, at her neighbors, Ron Delaney and Stan Field.

In an alcove to the right, the big guy with the beard came out shooting. He was hit in the shoulder and spun around, staggering, trying to stand, his shots going wild. Officer Diane Miller and a new face from the town of Valeria had entered from the back of the minivan, ready for anything that needed to be done. Rochelle Halliday lunged at Diane, immediately recognizing her from the magazine-cluttered table. "Bitch, you goddam bitch!" she said, spitting at her. "Get yer fuckin' hands off me," she said to Rob Delaney, "you shit, you rotten beast!" It took Rob and Diane and Stan to get her in handcuffs.

"Try to calm down, Mrs. Halliday," Stan said. "We have to get this operation finished, and we just broke that gate at the back where all the pretty green stuff is growing. Our chief honchos are on their way to close up your business and take all of you to the Sampson Quarry Police Headquarters that used to protect you."

"Sorry, honey, you blew it!" Diane said, with a sweet smile. "Now I have to go and use some Lysol to get your spit off my face."

The big car shop was surrounded, indoors and out. Lights flashed everywhere. Traffic on the highway was slowing, but was waved on. That area had not seen such a large operation or so many police in one place. When the entire surveillance team gathered, waiting for police wagons close by, their faces were beaming, flushed with satisfaction. "Hey, guys and gals, we need a couple of wagons to get this mob out of here. I'd say we used pretty good teamwork," Rob said. "Hope we have space in the paddy wagons for all this garbage."

VII.
September 2012

Betty and Fred Branson were driving back from a planned trip to seek out moving south when they stopped for lunch at McDonald's. Imelda had graduated from Michigan State, and was happily situated as a healthcare financial planner in New York. The Bransons had decided to relocate now that the "nest was empty," as they explained it. They began chatting with a friendly couple named Mattes who were driving to Connecticut when Betty mentioned Sampson Quarry. The couple immediately perked up when they heard the town's unusual name. "Isn't that the rural town in Ohio that made a name for itself with a crime scene...they were touted as smart and brave...some time ago?" the gentleman said.

"Yes," Betty said. "A drug operation was brought down, and we were proud of what we did. Some people would say we were 'the boonies' compared to the big towns, but we had the ability to stop a crime scene without a fatal casualty and just a real team spirit. One of our good neighbors was murdered because he was planning to go to the authorities because his wife was involved. She set her husband up for the murder. Yeah, she was quite a piece of work. She even suggested felt coverings for the killer's boots so that prints wouldn't be discovered. Up to a point she was smart, but it just took sharp eyes to find them. Even a little girl helped the police."

"Yes, yes, I remember now," Mr. Mattes said. "The woman was known across the country for her reaction when she was discovered. It was on TV. Didn't she attack a woman in the courthouse?"

"You got it," Fred said. "She resisted arrest, and she was violent. We learned that it took three people to handcuff her when she was caught. Even during the trial she screamed obscenities like a drunken sailor. Officer Diane gave evidence and pinned her down in the courthouse during the trial, and when she was taken away she broke free from the guards and punched Diane with a blow that knocked her to the ground. It didn't help her case, that's for sure. Diane had a black eye, but made a joke of it: 'It's my trophy.

If that's all I suffered helping to catch a creature like that, I don't mind a shiner.'

"The whole case was unusual in that the big guy took orders from Mrs. Halliday, even to murdering her husband. Everybody did. She was the kingpin. When he was up against it he cooperated, hoping for leniency, but they threw the book at him, and he won't be going anywhere soon. The jury was influenced by his wimpish behavior bowing down to her, adding to his murder conviction.

"The pair of 'em were planning to leave town just before they were caught. The big guy had kids in town, His kids didn't know what it was all about, and they were kicking up a fuss about leaving their friends. So the pair of them were careless about being seen."

"We heard that it was a real, honest-to-goodness ambush by the police that fixed 'em, right?" Mrs. Mattes said.

"I guess you could say that, but it was really a comrade-in-arms situation where all the neighboring police forces got together, and they were somehow so determined to get these people that nothing was leaked, and they grabbed them before they knew what was happening. We were proud of the police in all the surrounding towns, not just Sampson Quarry. A young rookie called Sampson Quarry from fifty miles away. He had hacked into a private cell phone and picked up conversations about shipments to the border, and to New York, New Jersey, you name it. He caught precise destinations. The kid almost put drop-off points and whereabouts of all the crime gang in the laps of his superiors. He was a true hero—along with the kids." Everybody enjoyed a good laugh.

"Well, we're proud to know you, folks," Mr. Mattes said. "How are things now after all these years? It seems it was a small town made of the right stuff, as they say."

"Yes," Betty stated. "It was a wonderful town that became broken. Pride was lost with the horrible crime destroying the happiness, you might say. Neighbours we loved became indifferent, even though we were proud of our crime stoppers. The children growing up all wanted to get away from the reputation of the town. The distraught Halliday sons were not even heard of after the trial. They had their property sold for them, from where nobody knew. We saw rapid changes—sad things, like shops closing and stuff. It seemed to us that it would become a ghost town, and we weren't far wrong. The one and only strip mall sported signs saying 'sellout sale,' etc., long ago.

"The owners of the town's busy service station, the Bertrand brothers, were part of the drug selling. They were cleaning up shop, getting ready to skip town on a nice, sunny day when our marvellous police officer, Diane Miller, who got the black eye, walked through the front door of their shop with her gun drawn. A couple of colleagues were waiting outside the door. Apparently she said, 'Goin' somewhere, guys?' The shop, which was once a thriving outlet for everything related to everybody's cars, closed down. They were indicted with the criminal couple, hauling in tons of money, even though the nice young folks employed there didn't know a thing until they were let go. Ironically, the burned-out car of the killer was taken to their shop. They played the actor game like pros, pretending to know nothing when the car was being examined. They even knew who it had belonged to.

"So the crime destroyed a town and saddened all the good people that once felt proud of their bustling little town. We are almost the last to go. We just sold our property, and we took a big loss. We're on our way back now to finalize the paperwork. The unusual makeup of a neat little town is now history."

"Thanks for sharing with us, folks," Mr. Mattes remarked. "It's the old story about a few rotten apples, isn't it? In this case they destroyed a way of life."

Part II
Poetry

Seeking the Solution to a Riddle
Wrapped in Mystery inside an Enigma

Our eyes see much and understand little.
We look to the Universe and we see what?
Sky.
What do we know about the sky?
 Let the moon and the stars enchant us.
We cannot be unfeeling.
But such a wondrous sight cannot be explained.
 What is beyond the beyond?
 Is the cosmos orderly, or is it chaotic?
We don't know. We are unable to know.
Can we describe the beginning or the passage of time?

From scientists we learn that every day makes Planet Earth less significant.
We have sent machines skyward for discovery.
Scraping the surface?
Not even close.
We do not yet know how life began.
The wise and the educated accept evolution.
Every clue shows us the inevitable.
Gradual change in molecular life has been obvious.
Creationism is naïve.
Millions of years have displayed the changing features of man and beast,
and everything else.

But there has to be another dimension.

Evolution indeed, but what force commands the changes?

Nobody can pretend that evolution is controlled by man.

No man helps an exquisite butterfly to emerge from its protective shroud.

No human hands unfurl the silken petals of a rose.

Caprice

(A Poem for a Thoughtful Child)

When the autumn rain comes down it is cold rain. It doesn't seduce us with velvet drops. Velvet drops come with warm spring rain.

And a little breeze that sweetens.

Cold rain is defiant, uncomfortable, harsh.

Raise one's face and it strikes, not with gentle touches, but with a determined force.

We are, in enlightenment, eager to wrap our arms around nature's whims.

The cold rain insults us, but we tell it that we understand.

It is disguised as wayward and mean, but we know better. It makes promises.

Any rain is enchanting, and it nurtures.

Its destiny is within the earth.

Soon small white and yellow blossoms will be impelled to push up through the comforting beds they have slept in. Happily, for them it's enough to feel the sunshine advancing, stirring life.

They speak to us: "See us. Smile at us. Love us."

And we do.

"Even when you were asleep we knew you were there. The prospects of your magic debuts made us feel close to you, even in your temporary slumber."

Promises kept.

The Path

I go to the path, a lively domain of runners early in the morning before sunshine takes away the night touch.... A branch has fallen. Aged, fanciful curves twisted, broken. When was it green and vigorous? Alone, thoughts wander....

A large figure ahead, surrounded by the heavy summer mist. It doesn't move like a runner. It simply doesn't move at all.... I slow my easy gait and watch a motionless being. Why does it stand still? I cannot approach....

My doorstep feels secure, but my mind is fixed on the path. In a curtained room I watch and wait. Joggers come and go, most in happy pairs.

I continue my day, but the vision doesn't leave me. Tomorrow? I'm not sure.

The branch is gone. The mist is there, shrouding the path, but no figure. I see it anyway.

I hold back. No, not now. There are other trails.... I run beside a wire fence. It is not appealing. Nature needs to accompany the avid runner. Not here.

I run the original path now, but not alone. I see the figure. It is not there, but I see it.

Nemesis?

Each of us is one of millions walking paths upon the earth.
When we look upon our legacy we have to doubt our worth.
We have left a trail of tragedy so wanton and perverse
That our egocentric interests seem to scorn the universe.

It would seem the human species has but avaricious bent;
Hate and greed and desecration are the values we present.
Most of us live life impassive, shreds of our potential good.
Why do trust and peace evade us? Can't we better what we should?

From primeval physiology has humankind improved,
Or was it evil nourishment that evolution moved?

Let us ponder for a moment—put aside the self-disgrace.
Let's objectively examine what compels the human race.

Every wild thing living freely has its predators to fear.
Each must flee or cower hidden when the enemy is near.
We accept this truth of fauna, yet we cannot do the same;
If we do not vanquish adversaries, frailty is our shame.

We cannot oppose diseases that have mysteries yet unknown,
And their latent threats defy us even when we're left alone.
We are plagued by heavy burdens that intensify and grow,
And we cling to preservation armed with only what we know.

We can only watch in terror as the storms and floods descend,
And from our innate beginnings we have known that life must end.
There are forces moving round us that we cannot comprehend.

Can we justify our errors or ourselves exonerate?
With complacent resignation can we blame our sins on fate?

No, we cannot, and we do not, for our work is never done.
We awake and venture forward with each rising of the sun.
As each day of life progresses and our instincts are employed
We accept a confrontation with a nameless, shapeless void.

We are given mental power fundamental to our creed.
Such awareness shows us clearly every cruel, destructive deed.
We could not deplore a history of facts we do not know.
Could exclusive right to reasoning be retribution's blow?

Mike, the Unimpeachable

(a very short story)

I saw him regularly but briefly.

The rabbit moved like a flash of sunlight. His coat was glossy, I think. Such speed can fool the eye.

I wanted him to look at me without fear.

It is a pity that gentle children and thoughtful adults cannot summon a wild thing to come near. How beguiling it would be if a little boy could touch, at will, the soft brow of a creature of innocence and beauty. It would be enrichment.

Alas, nature is wise. Animals flee. They must.

I named the rabbit Mike. I don't know why.

One day I approached quietly, kneeling on soft ground, surrounded by tall marsh grasses. I was determined to gain more than a fleeting glimpse of Mike. Time passed slowly before the quivering snout and big eyes silently appeared at the entrance to his domain, a grassy vent in the ditch. I think I did not breathe for the moment. Mike nibbled the grass, then hopped, just once, and continued to nibble.

In my silent delight I pondered and realized that I was thinking of the rabbit as a "he." Perhaps that was incorrect. I couldn't tell. The seasons of birth and infancy were past, and if Mike were a mother, the offspring would have scattered.

That thought soothed me.

The dark mini-cave would soon be Mike's security against the harsh winds to come.

I had to move my foot and a twig snapped.

Mike vanished before the sound had registered.

When the autumn winds were becoming bitter I wandered to Mike's home and saw "him" a few more times.

Frost became heavy. Mike no longer appeared.

I felt a loss. It bordered on loneliness.

I gave no thought to a coyote sighting near Mike's den. It was a given within my mind that Mike was sound asleep.

Deep within his den.

Ornicycle

Little birds gather and twitter.   Big birds soar.

```
 .'.'   ...".'.'  ,                      > > >   >
  '  .. ,, ..                              >     >
    .. ,,    ,..                          < <
      '  ." ."  .                            >
  ,..    ''''   ...                        > >   >
```

The leaves are falling. Worms and insects are going under ground

It's time to leave   Be safe
    and follow the sun.   and come back soon!

   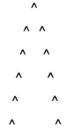

Part III

Experience/Opinion/Defiance

Guyana

1. The Place

When I was a young woman I was given the opportunity to live in a very unusual and exciting home for a year in the late fifties where only aboriginal natives had walked before. My husband, Douglas McLean, an American of Scottish ancestry, was asked to set up an assaying laboratory in the tropical rain forest of what was at the time called British Guiana. Doug was an analytical chemist, and he was asked to join a group of English mining engineers and geologists who were establishing a mine in the undeveloped terrain of the British colony, now known as Guyana after becoming independent in 1966. The goal was the procurement of manganese. There was a world shortage at the time of the important element for industry.

Guyana is located on the north shore of South America, and is one of three "Guianas," Dutch Guiana (Suriname), and French Guiana to the east.

The shorelines of these countries are not the usual Caribbean blue; they are opaque, and the color of chocolate milk, or even black in some areas. The torrential rains and subsequent runoff from the interior rivers and streams carry tannins from the vegetation that lives and dies in profusion in the interior. Growth and wildlife are incomparable in density and abundance.

We had travelled abroad often, and had spent several months in Africa following the same professional pursuits, but this endeavor was expected to be about a year living within the tropical rain forest. I was advised not to go because there was an insurrection at that time in Georgetown, the capital city. I wanted no part of the dire warnings and proceeded to Georgetown with my husband. We arrived a few days after two British warships anchored in the harbor.

Doug was chosen for this unusual venture because he was an excellent diplomat, having been schooled in Scotland, where he learned to have a deep appreciation for fair play and sportsmanship. It was clear that he also had the adventurous spirit of the "explorer" within his British psyche. I, too, was ready for whatever came about, probably with a strong mix of naiveté for the impending living in what was indeed the domain of the hunter-gatherer.

The trip to the camp took more than three days by seaplane, river boat, and Land Rover, followed by a seven-mile walk with a guide thereafter where clearing had not begun sufficiently for vehicles to be used. The camp was called Matthews Ridge, named after a geologist who was one of us. My house had a thatched roof, and was situated on long stilt-like poles for the expected rains and mudslides. The sides were corrugated aluminum.

2. Personnel

Our camp consisted of ten mining engineers and geologists. Our project manager, Jeff Lomas, had hired several Amerindians to do practical work and to gather food. My house boy was of mixed race with bright, dark skin and curly hair. My cook, of Portuguese descent, had his own small house close to my house—four poles with a thatched roof—and a rough propane stove within. A small pallet was his bed. When I asked him if he had any fear at night, he was quite taken aback. "No, no, not in my place. It's mine."

Two excellent workers were two older men who had been freed from Devil's Island. Sharpeau was a leper, and kept to the shadows when he wasn't working in the forest. Gustave had murdered a man in Buenos Aires. Both men received and sent mail to their native France, but were not allowed to return.

I remember one man well for his typical bearing and name so allied to the adventurous British history we all know. His name was Guy Ravenscroft. He was a mining engineer from "proper" public schooling in England, and he was a good sport, probably because his colleagues had put him in his place from the start by telling us that he had applied in London for the job in a bowler hat and spats—on his way to the jungle.

My husband was the only chemist, and I was the only woman. We were a motley crew.

3. Guyana Now

Guyana is a paradox. The warm climate that produces beautiful flowers and trees near the more developed city thoroughfares and commercial dwellings is negated by the land's being under sea level. This fact keeps developers away, with no gemlike colors in the waves of the Caribbean lapping at its shores. Ironically, the underdevelopment keeps gaudy tourist ventures from moving in, and thus leaves much of it as nature decrees. The country is indeed a rough diamond, with magnificent towering trees in its interior realm where even butterflies are thrilling. The wild and natural space could best be appreciated by approaching the wisdom of Shakespeare's descriptive genius. In *The Tempest*, Miranda speaks to her father in these words: "There is nothing ill can dwell in such a temple." Her subject was a handsome man, but the words fit for our temple, which was dense greenery topped by a canopy of very tall trees.

No, perhaps nothing ill can dwell in such a place until the hand of man encroaches. Nobody can forget the infamous Jonestown massacre. The hideous crime took place at our camp, and the shootout that took place, killing a Congressman and several others took place at Port Kaituma, where we had met the driver of the Land Rover years before. Also, it seems that now there is a railway to Matthews Ridge. It is said to be dangerous now to be in the vicinity because of drug sales and other crimes.

It would take a very lengthy book to cover the many experiences we had in that extraordinary and mystical place. In brief passages I cannot tell realistically of the insurrection that took place at the time in the capital city, and I cannot describe in detail what we ate and how we kept clean. Nor can I describe properly the appearances of snakes and tarantulas, but a brief episode or two can help to describe the seldom-reached interior of a rain forest. There are still feelings of pride, fear, and amazement within me. Two of them follow, one a fearful experience with a snake, and the other a source of joy with a feathered companion.

4. The Night of the Bushmaster

I was never unduly frightened of snakes as some are, but we did experience many in the camp. Most often encountered was the bushmaster. The bushmaster is a reptile of the pit viper class, such as a rattlesnake, but larger. It is considered the largest venomous snake in the Americas. Some reach more than ten feet. (I had never heard of one until I arrived in Guyana.) They were killed, of course. Fortunately we have learned that this is not a sensible approach in our day.

We came upon a bushmaster when it happened to be New Year's Eve. My husband and I were on our way with kerosene lamps in hand to the Mess Hall. Interesting spirits had been sent from Georgetown for the holiday eve celebration. Nothing could be chilled, of course, so we didn't expect fine white wine or the like, but we were excited and ready for fun.

The snake was straddling the path in a gully we had to cross. We had to race back to our house, a hundred yards away, to figure out what to do. Doug used a large stick to bash the aluminum siding of our house several times to get the attention of the men at the Mess Hall. It seemed idiotic, but it worked. We soon saw flashlights coming toward us. We could not let anybody walk into the path of the snake, so we had to run back and warn them. We screamed through the dark of night, "Snake, snake, just ahead of you!" Three gunshots followed shortly, and we proceeded toward the lights. When we gathered we found that it was not the same snake. It was smaller and darker in color. We knew bushmasters well, and some of the native men showed me the fangs of some that had been killed.

The big snake roamed freely for the rest of our stay at Matthews Ridge. It was sighted by two people without firearms, but never destroyed.

I watched a nature film on television not long ago wherein a naturalist was seeking a bushmaster in Brazil and getting discouraged. I could have told him to go to Georgetown, take a few days to get up river to Port Kaituma and turn right.

5. Gumdrop

One day to my delight I hurried outside to the call of two young men who had a present for me. Everybody knew by my conversations that I had a strong reverence for the natural world, particularly prominent in the tropical flora and fauna about us. I had told everybody in the camp of my enjoyment of the wildlife, and having seen flocks of fascinating birds, the camp had taken notice. "For you, Mistress," one of the boys said. He held a small green parrot on his forefinger. Two shiny dark eyes in a swath of green feathers were staring at me. I fell in love with the little creature at sight. It was a female "Amazon green," the boys told me. They beamed at me with flashing white teeth when they saw my look of pure joy. The little thing stepped directly onto my finger. I walked up the wooden stairs with her and looked back to tell them as they walked away smiling, "I love her already. Thank you so much!"

I took her inside to get a good look. She appeared to be quite happy. In fact, she was uncanny; I placed her on a table, and she walked immediately toward me, made her way up my arm, and perched on my shoulder. Her name was fore-ordained; she was small, round, and green. "Gumdrop" was perfect. She became my very important companion. Her wings had been clipped, and I lamented the handicap it made for her. But she would have flown at any time if she had been able, and she ate and rested and demanded my attention constantly as time passed, appearing to be completely happy as a companion.

Doug built her a cage with a perch inside to roost on. He also built a small ladder on our front porch railings. She climbed the ladder several times, and then she walked into her cage and got up on the roost. She seemed to say immediately, "Thanks, but what's the big deal?"

We bedded her down each day at dusk in her cage hanging from a hook on our back porch. I worried about her safety for a while, but found that she was quite alright. If we went to her after she was settled she had a low growling sound that told us to leave her alone. She wanted to sleep. Every morning my houseboy took her out of her cage because she was scolding Doug and me for sleeping past six.

In daylight, when a cloudburst was coming after a lull, she knew it. She scurried outside where she fluffed out her feathers, spreading them outward, shrieking with joy, the rain falling on her in torrents. She also knew danger. At times a low, deep sound came from her as she looked skyward. In seconds hawks or eagles flew above. She saw them before we did.

My time in the challenging jungle was made easier by a little bird. I had seen nature in its most demanding forms; i.e., pounding rain, brilliant sunshine, tropical heat, deafening sounds from creatures in the forest, and growth that seemed overpowering, but the company of a small, intelligent creature helped me feel that I was needed while all the men worked all day and I was left to my own devices.

Two Men and a Baby

Discussions these days are often concerned with personal topics that were rarely considered in mixed company half a century ago. They should have been, but even with improvements erasing various ill-conceived practices from the past, some abominations have remained. They have, in fact, become subjects for politicians to exaggerate or lie about for whatever group they want to cajole. Knowing this, I hereby move on to an experience which altered my future drastically when I was a young woman. It was a long time ago, but it has memories that are a part of me, and in reality it could and does happen today to many.

There are several synonyms for the word *receptacle* in Roget's Thesaurus; i.e., container, receiver, vessel, etc. I was one of those items more than fifty years ago. I became pregnant. I was happily married, and my husband and I exulted in my pregnancy. I had never felt better. There was no morning sickness, and I had energy to spare. It was the greatest joy I had ever known.

After an examination a couple of months later, my obstetrician handed me a note to give to the nurse at the front desk. On the way I read the note: *Arrange X-Rays for possible congenital anomaly*. I immediately knew something was wrong. My hands were shaking when I handed the note to the nurse and asked her what it meant. She took some time and looked around before she responded. "I think the baby's probably just small because you are," she said, smiling. I was wary, however, because she seemed flustered. It was also a questionable explanation. She said she would inform me of the X-ray appointment.

I was still uneasy when I arrived home. I called my brother-in-law, who was also a physician, to question him about the note. He told me not to worry, that it was probably of no consequence. "It's your first baby," he said, "and we don't know how things will be. It's still early." The two doctors talked. The two doctors made the decision to let nature take its course, even though they knew that there was no hope for a natural birth and little chance for the baby's survival.

As time went by, my husband and I began to excitedly prepare a nursery with playful animal pictures on the walls. With the sex unknown, I set aside the classic pink or blue and covered a tiny bassinette with white satin and sunny yellow ribbon. A trace of fear stayed with me, ever so slightly dampening my exhilaration in knowing that I would soon become a mother. I adored my unborn child.

In the fourth month I had felt the flutter of life. After that the baby appeared exceptionally active. In the later stages the head was located near my waistline, unlike a natural pre-birth placement, and it seemed to me to be too large. Then, after nine months and nine days I began a fourteen-hour struggle with a breech delivery, at which time the nurses had to clamp my extremities because of my agony. The baby's hyperactivity continued throughout the labour, and my baby boy died during the birth process. He had spina bifida and hydrocephalus. Spina bifida is a deformity wherein a neural tube does not close up in the formation of the spinal cord, affecting not only the spine but the brain. It occurs during the first four weeks of pregnancy. The head enlargement was from the excessive accumulation of cerebrospinal fluid in the brain.

Some misbegotten people have stated that the fetus feels pain at an early stage, and thus should preclude any consideration of terminating the pregnancy. If that is the case, if my baby had been able to, he would have been screaming as the pregnancy advanced. The head enlargement from the fluid in the brain would have caused my baby pain worse than mine, even before the torturous herniation which occurred during delivery. Only the extremely ignorant would consider the development of pain in a fetus equal to that of a full-term baby. That is stating that God wills that one should continue a deformed four-week pregnancy to await the pain and suffering of an abnormal and excruciatingly painful birth and atrocious ending of a baby's life.

When my sedation wore off my family was at my bedside with the hideous news. But there was more. The burial arrangements were made without me because I was tired and distraught. Later, foolishly, I was determined to see the burial site. I was in hysterical shock when I saw a crude mound of earth in a cemetery near a factory—in a slag heap.

It was only a woman who read the doctor's crudely inept note. How could she understand big, medical words? It was only a woman who had to wait for a fetus to become a person. Time has softened the impact of the anguish forced upon my child and me. Yet I seethe within when I hear ignorant fools sounding forth so many years later—now, this very day, putting women in the category of sheep or goats, off-handedly subjugating them, patronizingly determined to govern and regulate what they consider to be the reproductive organs of an inferior sex. There were many more mounds in that slag heap.

Would a lost embryo, however lovingly anticipated, leave the same everlasting heartbreak as a baby? Would an undeveloped embryo suffer the same excruciating pain as a developing, compromised baby? No, they are not the same.

Many would condemn me for suggesting the premise of choice. I believe, and I pray. For those who bother to read or look at the world beyond their self-important circles, they would see thousands of third world children with vacant eyes, distended bellies, and infections of every sort, flies surrounding them. Are we to believe that this is God's will? Must we believe that God forced them into the world to suffer and die? Can we see Him in the eyes of dying children too much in pain to cry? To say it is God's will is to blame God for ordering them to be conceived and to die in pain. I don't think that was His desire for life on earth. It is man and woman, not God, who conceive life, often through pitiful ignorance, without thought for the consequences of the child-to-be. Or, it is the "fate" of most women (yes, more than 60 percent) on our planet to be subjugated to accepting pregnancy whether or not it is their wish. Many are, indeed, receptacles.

I am certain that God would want those who can alleviate suffering to do so. If the blind-sided would reach further than their pretentious holiness, they might look into the real world that exists beyond their comfortable lives.

For those who sorely need education in reality, pick up your iPad and check out the World Health Organization. Every year 303,000 women in developing countries die from pregnancy-related causes. That is more than 25,250 every month, or more than 840 each day. Also, 5.6 million children died in 2016 before the age of five. This was from the poor health of the mothers, malnutrition, disease, and world indifference to the many who live in filth. These are facts, even with foundations and private people trying to make headway in health care while battling cruel political obstacles along the way. One could not make up such horror. The poor and the deprived are disdained, treated as lowlifes of no consequence because they are far away. Living in the same world as those pitiful souls, the affluent cultures which we know and to which they aspire could give them greater wisdom regarding birth control, pursuing help for them by teaching them. Instead, many who live in comfort unthinkingly demand that embryos be protected, even if the "receptacle" of the zygote is a twelve-year-old rape victim.

One has to question the sanity of women in particular who carry large placards confronting Planned Parenthood facilities that offer much-needed help for forsaken and lonely women, or simply women who need help in examinations for chronic and terrifying conditions. Those sign-wielders are beyond contempt, and they have to be singularly stupid. Considerate voices could go a long way toward teaching the overwhelming number of women in need that their bodies are their own. They cannot value themselves if they are not valued. It would be wise to teach them by example how not to conceive babies that will have to be neglected and unprepared for a difficult world.

Some vociferous men and women even pretend magnanimity by indulging women whose lives may be in danger in pregnancy—"allowing" them abortions to save their lives. Why? If the mother-to-be is just a temporary holding bin of little consequence, why not just preach the ill-advised sermon about pro-life and let her die?

Within our modern world the mindset still remains in many forms, putting women in a herd category, incapable of intelligent pursuits. And those who pretend piety don't know what they are talking about, nor do they care.

If one can read, then read! Compare the reality to the ignorant incantations of some high-profile people who so unfortunately make laws.

To the charlatans who preach, I'm ready for you.

Our Universal House of Cards

God is master of all to many. But whether or not we follow scripture, the gifts of the earth are impossible to understand with just common sense and the ability to see and hear. We are drawn to the unfathomable, often frustrated by what we can't understand. It follows that we often feel that there must be a Supreme Power. We embrace intense feelings of love, but we cannot see love. Experience is a profound asset which we cherish, but it cannot be touched. It is intangible. Who has made a hummingbird? From where does the crystal stream flow? The hardest person would treasure a lush meadow after a storm with drops of rain glistening on flowers. We did not scatter those gems of life. Can we look at a towering redwood tree and say that we gave it permission to grow? Evolution should no longer be questioned. It is universally accepted. However, something is missing; who or what directs the obvious changes?

What have we been doing since we walked upright? We have not solved the mysteries mentioned above, but we should treasure them and be grateful. However, in the thousands of years that mankind has existed on our beautiful planet we should have gained community understanding and love for others. Many animals became sociable, taking from the earth only what they needed for survival. We reached some forms of camaraderie, but over time, unfortunately, the hominid lost his way.

Let us think of what we have and how we use it. The oceans are vast, and countless creatures come to us from therein to sustain us. The growth of plant life is endless. Animals of infinite form live with us. Thus food and sustenance come to us in profusion from the seas, from the trees, and on the ground, ordered to do so by the sun above us. Billions of worthy creatures have nurtured us. The great wealth of growth and perpetuation of life in the past have given us the future in which we now live. The flora and fauna have been and continue to be harvested and captured, perhaps with energy and hard work creating propagation, but perpetual seeding and animal husbandry are pursued only for our own uses. We take from all directions, but we have difficulty giving back.

Innocence also has been secure only in the animal kingdom; the mightiest beast is free from evil. He has taken care only of himself and his progeny since he first roamed the earth. Unfortunately we, the people, have evolved into severely flawed beings.

The oceans that wrap around the continents and the rivers and streams are dumping grounds for us. The refuse and the toxic are tossed in. Plastic of every shape and size stretch now on the great expanses for many miles, and tons are pouring in daily in every part of the globe, destroying wildlife and polluting water even for our own consumption. The governmental plans for cleanup are insipid. Political beings seek improvement only if their lobbying partners allow them to.

The trees that make great forests and harbor homes for wildlife and endless offerings for the health of the environment are being stripped to the ground beneath for agriculture. Construction is progressing rapidly with the planning of edifices and luxury homes and playgrounds, and anything that will please the inhabitants as we swallow up nature with impunity.

It is ironic that history has given us genuine heroes. Some people during famine and disease and war have given their altruistic selves to serve those who need help. Philanthropy is well known in some industry and in personal largesse, for which we should be thankful. We feel pride when tragedies are followed by people who rush to offer their talents to ease suffering. But billions of people now inhabit the planet, and the greatest of offerings are not enough to make heartfelt changes in the lot of the countless unfortunate souls who do not have enough food or health care or shelter. It's a pity that the majority doesn't have the virtue of some.

We have blithely invented grotesque weapons. Even if our planet is not destroyed in one fell swoop, slow, insidious destruction will do the job. Wars will continue while life on earth exists. With the deep coveting within us there can be no peace on earth; there never was and there never will be. Obsessive human traits are supremely invulnerable. Greed and all of the deadly sins are paramount and impermeable in most human beings. The human simply has thwarted peace and exploited the gifts of nature since he began making tools.

Those of us who inhabit the earth today live under the threat of nuclear destruction which we modeled with our intelligence telling our hands what to do. In modern times machine guns and flame-throwers were pretty good weapons. Hand grenades and bombs were sufficiently evil. Then came the nuclear age. The possibility of annihilation still lurks in the large accumulation of hideous inventions. The threat of the mushroom clouds is very much alive, although the anxiety did lessen somewhat through familiarity as the years passed. The Cold War threatened us when two superpowers were using the stockpiling of atom bombs and ballistic missiles to exhibit strength. With a welcome thaw in the relationship of the great Eastern Empire and its nemesis called "The West," intimidation became a little more reasonable. A wall fell and a Union came apart. However, threats became more deadly along the way when less advanced people were getting into the act. "Me too" was the idiotic demand for nuclear weapons from heavily-populated countries wherein most of their people were neglected, starving or diseased, and perpetually breeding. The demand stands today and creeps further.

The more advanced nations create an indefensible position. They buy power. Those who politically hold the stage must be rich, or beholden to the rich, and those who associate with them generally keep close; the advantages are alluring and beneficial no matter what the cost in pride and character. Fabricated stories from corrupt politicians often please the ignorant, while ignorance expands in a constantly polarizing state. The speeches reap fear in voters in order to lure them into falsehoods. Leadership, therefore, becomes artificial. Yes, we have seen corporate mega-wealth buy elections to government office. And the ready access to protective loopholes shields the wealthy from consequences. We hear of philanthropy and genuine compassion in some of the very wealthy people, but even their admirable help is no match for the great number of less worthy – those who have everything they could possibly need, but continue to obsess over possessions, and feel that the good fortune is their due. In their infinite comfort on high they are not likely to give anything away.

Deterioration could proceed, ironically, from poverty and from wealth. The wretched of no means could slowly lose direction and goals, breeding from natural instincts and using nature's bounty to prolong slow dissolution, while the rich would covet more and take what they want while it exists. Both classes could be equally guilty of the loss, the poor through grasping for life and the rich from natural gluttony.

From the Neanderthal to the present day man has destroyed or taken from every gift the earth brings forth. Even believing that God is master, in His name man has been, according to genuine history, the vicious, the cruel, the strong debasing the weak. In the name of the Lord religions have exacted indescribable horror with bombs, machetes and in some cases the pursuit of extermination by any means at hand. There is no limit to the loathing of man to man or the lengths some human cults would go in acts of barbarism. For many people guns and other instruments of death are toys.

If we were to revisit the souless history of our race from primeval times, there would be very little honesty in suggesting that we have come a long way. We have not. If God does indeed see all, He has been defeated.

Throughout history life has been blessed now and then with good people that have changed the world. We have to find those with character and integrity and pursue optimism. Capitulation is despair. Let us defeat despair. I think that some day there will be a reckoning.

Gens du monde, gardez la foi!

Epilogue

Within these pages I wish to clarify my revelations about humanity. Some of my passages appear extreme. Often female chauvinism is apparent. However, too many of us are too eager to criticize leaders and political situations without examining ways to change things. Awakening to the evil and the injustice is becoming pronounced in some circles, fortunately, but there is still too much work to be done to make life fair, or even bearable for those who are trapped in hopeless misery and indifference. Far away? Of course. Yet many are at our very doorsteps needing help. It's the epitome of selfishness to feel that they should take care of themselves when often circumstances forced them into degradation, and they simply could not survive without help.

There has been a surge of acceptance of women's voices and opinions regarding needed progress, not long ago considered of little value – not to be taken seriously. I believe that surge is getting stronger, and I exult in the sources of many aspects of change; together with women seeking political office and pursuits beyond the caretaking of others, bright, professional men are vocally advocating the hopes and dreams of women. God bless those of you who hear us.

Within you, the prominent sex, is the power to help us along. We welcome your sheltering arms, and we will be ready to offer our own when we approach equality.

I was assisted in computer procedures by a talented
friend, Mark Zielinski. His patience was outstanding.